MW01075888

MILK AND HONEY

A World War II Biographical Saga

WRITTEN BY

GREGORY J. BAYER

STORY BY ERICH BAYER

Bublish

Mt. Pleasant, SC

Copyright © 2019 by Gregory J. Bayer

All rights reserved. No part of this publication may be reproduced, distributed or transmitted in any form or by any means, without prior written permission.

Gregory J. Bayer

315 Titusville Road

Poughkeepsie, NY 12540

Publisher's Note: This is a work of nonfiction. Names, characters, places, and incidents are a product of the author's best memory.

Book Layout © 2019 BookDesignTemplates.com

Editing/Cover Design/Distribution by Bublish, Inc.

ISBN 978-1-64704-167-0 (Paperback)

ISBN 978-1-64704-168-7 (eBook)

Dedicated to our mother Marianne, the love of our Dad's life, and my two brothers, Chris and Mark.

"No man is a failure who has friends!"

Clarence the Angel, *It's a Wonderful Lif*

CONTENTS

CHAPTER ONE

Crooked Path

Food! At my fingertips is all the food I could ever want. I will never be hungry again. I have just returned from my honeymoon. I'm up early and standing in front of my fully stocked refrigerator. As it does from time to time, it strikes me that I can eat whatever I want and as much as I want. I have truly made it! For much of my childhood, finding food was a daily challenge. The word *hungry* doesn't really do justice to the sensation that was perpetually present in my life for years. It is a memory that will shape the rest of my life.

I work for International Business Machines (IBM) in the research department, putting my skills as a tool and die maker to good use. IBM is just about to get into advanced computer machinery, and I am an integral part of this cutting-edge environment. I can finally fulfill the promise I made to my father as we were standing on the pier in Bremerhaven, Germany, just a few years earlier, to make my family proud.

The path I took to get to this point was not straight by any means. My life, and the lives of the rest of my family, could have been snuffed out at any time during World War II. It wasn't until I was standing there in my kitchen that it really hit me--I now had all the abundance I could only imagine back then.

I am the product of a long-distance relationship, kindled during the early stages of war preparation, that was made more difficult by the national fervor that gripped the country. I was born in Nuremburg, Germany, in 1935 to parents who had just met...a chance encounter, you might say.

In December 1934, my father, Johann Bayer, was a freshly-minted soldier in the German army. Along with some friends, he had decided to attend a Christmas dance one especially frigid Saturday night. It was sponsored by the German equivalent of the USO, Amstgruppe für Wehrmachtpropaganda(the WPr, part of the propaganda effort for nationalism). My mother, Lisa Bieswanger, was a teenaged volunteer who'd gotten caught up in the national effort to bolster morale among the troops. Her duties included knitting wool socks, writing letters to soldiers, and working at the weekend dances.

As fate would have it, Lisa was serving refreshments when Johann wandered by to quench his thirst. The immediate electricity felt between the two was palpable. The dance hall was brimming with excitement as soldiers on R&R, or just with the night off, crowded into the church basement to blow off some steam, drink, and perhaps, if lucky, win a dance with a local girl.

Johann walked in to the hall with some buddies and took up residence at a large table. They were all sharply dressed in their unforms, their pants pressed and shoes buffed. They looked commanding and confident. It was still early and the hall was beginning to fill. The five-piece jazz band was mintues away from finishing their preparations. After a few minutes, you could just sense the soldiers were getting a bit ansty. Johann suggested a round of beers and volunteered to fetch them.

He made his way over to the concessions and was suddenly taken with a particular fraulein. He had very little experience interacting with the fairer sex, so he felt a bit tongue-tied. He stammered out a weak hello, and the girl returned a demure smile that left him captivated. She was wearing a simple flowered dress, her blonde hair hung just below her shoulders, and she was wearing just a hint of pink lipstick. He thought he caught a hint of jasmine perfume. She poured him several cold beers and handed them to him without a word. They locked eyes for what may have been only a second, but something immediately clicked, or at least he thought so. As he handed over the cash, her hand slightly brushed against his and his heart jumped. *What was that?* he thought.

As he walked away, it was as if his head was on a swivel, continually rotating to catch a glimpse of that smile as she served the hordes of thirsty soldiers. Johann sat back down, unsuccessfully hiding his change in demeanor from his friends. As young men (boys, really) have a penchant to do, they egged him on. They teased, chided, and cajoled him until he had gathered enough courage (and had imbibed enough beer) to go back and speak with her.

His moment came when there was a bit of a lull in the line. He got up from the table with a half-empty beer stein and took a circuitous route, as if he was gathering his confidence. He stopped and greeted a few friends on the other side of the room, laughing at a couple of jokes while glancing back at the beer line as if planning his attack. Finally, he'd had enough. He threw his shoulders back, lifted his head, and marched over to the kitchen. Before he lost his courage, he went right to the front of the line and blurted out, "Could I have the next dance?"

At first, she was surprised by the forwardness of it all, but she replied without thinking. "Of course!" she said. "I get a break in a few minutes, so wait for me by the stage."

As he walked away with a huge smile on his face, she yelled out, "I'm Lisa, by the way."

She was self-assured for a girl so young. She stood about 5'5", slender of stature with radiant blonde hair and blue eyes that stirred something in him down to his toes. He did as he was told. Like clockwork, she appeared through the crowd and his heart went into overdrive. He got up from the table with just the proper amount of friendly prodding from his friends. A bit of perspiration appeared on his temples. Thankfully, the music was loud, making conversation impossible. He asked her if she would like to dance and she quickly agreed. He politely positioned his right hand on the small of her back with enough authority to render confidence without appearing overly pushy.

She immediately felt his strength. His breath was minty, with a hint of beer. With her right hand in his left, she developed the impression that his fingers were soft, not calloused, the mark of a man who used his brain. Straight away, she was taken by his presence. He was slightly taller than her, but powerfully built, with broad shoulders and a strong chin.

At just 17 years old, Johann had enlisted in the army during Chancellor von Hindenburg's tenure, while Germany was under the regime of the Weimar Republic. He did so mostly because he didn't like the career his father had handpicked for him. In his youth, it was common for a father to have a heavy influence on his son's career path, especially if he knew someone in a business who needed an apprentice. My grandfather, Johann Bayer, Sr. (Hans for short), had a friend who owned an upholstery business. One Sunday morning, in a local pub over a tall beer, Johann's future was decided, or at least, so it seemed. Unfortunately for my grandfather, his son wanted nothing to do with the upholstery industry. He dreamed of being an automotive mechanic, and in his opinion, a career in upholstery was a long, hard road to nowhere. He reluctantly made his wishes known to his father, knowing full well his news would be received as an act of disrespect. His father would hear none of it.

Rather than go against his father's wishes, he did the only honorable thing at the time…he enlisted in the army. Because he was underage, he needed his father's permission. Instead of being disappointed that his son hadn't gratefully embraced the preordained upholstery apprenticeship, Hans stated unequivocally that he was proud of his son's choice and immediately signed off. His father believed being a soldier would make a man out of his son.

Although Germany was at peace at the time, the government was quietly rebuilding its army, despite the restrictions placed on it after the Treaty of Versailles, which was signed at the culmination of World War I. Who could have guessed a radical politician named Adolf Hitler was gaining fame and would soon be appointed chancellor by Hindenburg at the behest of his confidants? Despite the peaceful intermission, the army was eager to have my dad. The sour taste of war still clung to the tongues of Germany's youth. After the customary ten-week indoctrination and boot camp in Berlin, he was summarily assigned to the motorized unit, driving trucks. Ironically, he did not become a mechanic, but rather was trained to be a truck driving instructor.

He could have been stationed anywhere in Germany, but as fate would have it, he found himself right back in his home town of Nuremberg.

Now his destiny was about to be altered in a big way.

Time stood still. Despite their lack of experience in matters of the opposite sex, Johann and Lisa could not take their eyes off each other. The couple went from the dance floor to a table, mixing tantalizing banter with intimate dancing to the slower numbers. Neither was even aware of anyone else in the room. Conversation came easily.

Towards the end of the night, and before Johann's curfew, they got up from the table, and without so much as a word, made their way to a friend's car. They stood there for what seemed like an eternity as they gazed into each other's eyes.

Their first kiss was a mix of inexperience and clumsiness coupled with unbridled passion. Whether it was his crisp uniform, magnanimous personality, or forbidden good looks, Lisa would never quite understand why she fell so hard and so fast. It was out of character for her. But before fully comprehending the moment, they ended up in the back seat together. The awkwardness of removing clothes in such a tight space was quickly replaced by desire and basic instinct.

This chance encounter, as it so often does, led to an unexpected and unwanted result.

CHAPTER TWO

Finding Her Way

It wasn't long before my mother realized what was happening to her body. The hard part was going to be telling her family. She had just turned the tender age of eighteen and was going to have a baby with a man in the army, a man she hardly knew. The first challenge would be to actually find this debonair yet mysterious soldier. The second would be to figure out a way to tell her family she was pregnant.

She felt isolated, not knowing what to do next nor whom to turn to for advice. Her immediate fear was being shunned by her family and friends. The notion of an out-of-wedlock baby was one thing, but then trying to explain not knowing where the father was or how to find him was more than Lisa thought her family could handle. It was daunting, too, given the political direction the country was now heading and the now looming prospect of another war. The stress in her house from all of these unknowns was palpable, and Lisa knew she would only be piling on.

It became clear that she had to say something. At the time, Lisa still lived at home. She was one of five children--three sisters (Lisa, Wilma, and Freida) and two brothers (Paul and Johann). It was a cramped house, and it was about to feel even smaller.

One night, Lisa confided in her sisters. At first they were incredulious, but they quickly understood her plight. They encouraged her to tell their mother.

Surprisingly, her mother was more sympathetic than Lisa thought possible. It could have been her Gypsy uprbringing or just motherly love, but either way, Lisa was relieved.

Unfortunately, my grandfather was not at all understanding and was harsh in his condemnation. He felt it was a betrayal of the family honor. The winds of war were beginning to blow both in the house and in the countryside.

"Who was this soldier, and how could you let this happen, Lisa?" her father raged. "Look at the shame you have brought upon this family!" There was no consoling the man. He felt as most fathers do, given similar circumstances. He blamed himself, and it came across to his daughter as disappointment in her.

To make matters worse, Lisa could not answer her father's questions.

Lisa spent the first two weeks after this calamity going from crying in the arms of her sisters to blindly wandering the streets of the city, lost in heavy thoughts about her future. It was during one of these walks that she recognized a soldier from that fateful evening.

She ran up to him and he immediately recognized her, too. He spoke before she could blurt out one word.

"Oh My God…I cannot believe I bumped into you! I don't know if you remember me, but I'm Ludwig. You are all my friend Johann talks about. He is driving everyone in the company mad with his incessant talks of this blonde bombshell he met at the dance. Do you know what you have done to this poor soul?"

Shocked at this news, Lisa's face flushed crimson with embarrassment. She meant something to him! This was too good to be true. Had this stranger eased her burden just a bit? "Yes, what a coincidence. So good to see you, too. Of course I remember you. I would love to see Johann again! Do you know how I can find him?"

"I'm in a hurry. I have to get back to the base. But I guess you could give me your address and I'll be sure I get it to him."

Lisa walked home that day with a spirit as light as a cloud. She knew she loved Johann, and that's what troubled her more than anything. Of course she wanted a father for her baby, but she also wanted her soulmate. Now maybe it would all fall into place, especially if she could get her father on the same page as the rest of her family. What a relief!

On an icy and dismal Saturday afternoon in late March there was a knock on the door. As was customary in the house, the mother of the house answered the door. Just like that, Johann waltzed back into Lisa's life. He came courting with a small bouquet of flowers and a box of chocolates. Pretty extravagant for a military man!

He was cordially greeted by my grandmother as they both introduced themselves. Despite the circumstances, it was not as frosty in that hallway as it was outside.

Throughout the stiff but affable formalities of meeting Lisa's entire family, Johann had the uneasy feeling he was being closely scrutinized. Lisa anxiously waited until the first break in conversation and then whisked him out to the back yard for some privacy.

He had not forgotten about her. In fact, he eagerly divulged that she had occupied all of his thoughts and he could not believe how fate had brought them back together again.

"I cannot believe I found you again! What are the chances? I've had a hard time concentrating on any of my tasks throughout the day because you're all I think about."

"I know! Thank God I ran into Ludwig. I missed you so much, too!"

Alone in the shadows of the chilly garden, they shared a warm embrace. Standing outside and shivering for what seemed an eternity, she was looking for a way to break the news. How would a young soldier react to the news that a one-night stand had resulted in the girl before him being *in a family way*?

Before the heartfelt moment faded and she lost her nerve, she blurted out, "I'm pregnant!"

He stood there, speechless. She was waiting for a reaction, any reaction. As shocked as he was, he immediately requested her hand in marriage. He even got down on one knee. He was in love and would have it no other way.

What a gentleman, Lisa immediately thought. What a relief!

She said, "YES," without thinking. He stood up and lifted her off the ground with the intensity and strength of his bear hug.

"My knight in shining armor has come through," she whispered in his ear.

She wouldn't be a social outcast, after all!

However, as these two young lovers would soon learn quite well, things are never as easy as they appear. Once the moment had passed, he told her there might be military challenges to getting married. He was about to be deployed to a base near Berlin. He didn't know what the procedures were or how to go about it, but he would seek permission from his superiors to get married as soon as possible and find out whether it could be expedited. They had to get married right away.

They quickly went back in and announced their pending nuptials to the family. The atmosphere in the house swiftly defrosted. My once grumpy grandfather broke out a rare bottle of whiskey and made a toast. Smiles filled the kitchen.

Then, just as quickly as he had reappeared, Johann slipped back out the door and vanished again for another month. He wrote two letters chronicling his progress, or lack thereof, but they weren't a substitute for his promise.

To Johann's dismay, the army was not as understanding or as fast-acting as he had hoped. The Wehrmacht (headquarters) had more pressing matters to deal with than a star-crossed couple. The government was secretly reconstructing the country's military machine and preparing for war, although it wasn't apparent to those in its wake just yet.

Joahann finally received an official letter from Army Headquaters. It read, "Permission denied!"

In fact, an official letter from Hitler himself, the newly ordained *Führer* or *leader,* came through military channels forbidding the bond. The letter explained that married infantry soldiers were less valuable than their single brethren. Hitler, who had been appointed Chancellor by this point, required as many unattached troops as possible. Unbeknownst to the public at large, plans for a sweeping European invasion were well underway.

Johann was distraught. How would he explain this to the woman he loved and who was about to have his baby? The bad news consumed him. It was a particularly wet and dreary day as he sat down in the mess hall and contemplated how to best explain this to Lisa. His long, painful letter detailed the predicament and asked her to wait for him. It was sincere and sentimental, but Lisa's (and her family's) disappointment was palpable.

At least it was an official denial by the *Führer* himself, which slightly diluted Lisa's pain and displeasure, but it did little to squelch the vicious scuttlebutt of such a social black mark. Ultimately, she was still facing the world as an unwed mother. She was forlorn, to say the least. Devastated was closer to the truth. How was she to show her face in public, especially as her growing belly began to show? Back then, German society was not as unforgiving or judgmental as other countries were, but there was still a social price to pay. Although she wouldn't be a public pariah, she would certainly cast a wider shadow. The internal family struggle was just as much if not more of a challenge.

CHAPTER THREE

The Arrival

Into the world I came, regardless of family approval or social acceptance. My mother went into labor late in the evening of August 15, 1935. The midwife was called in as active labor became too much for Lisa to manage alone. The midwife arrived slightly after midnight. With the whole family gathered to bear witness, I made my appearance with a wailing cry that woke the neighborhood in the wee hours of the 16th. It was a hot and sticky summer, and it was not just the temperature-that had reached a boiling point.

A rather large assembly was held at the Nuremberg parade grounds a month after my birth. It was called "The Rally of Freedom," and it was another type of new arrival. It was the birth of the Nazi Party on a national level.

It was a huge display of political and military prowess. The stadium held close to 50,000 spectators and was at near capacity. Hitler stood at the top of a podium ordained with a Swastika (a symbol appropriated to represent the Nazi Party), regaled in all his uniformed splendor. The crisp creases of his pants billowed in the breeze. Troops as far as the eye could see came marching in mechanic unison, turning their heads and saluting him with an outstretched hand and the mandatory, "Heil Hitler!" He was a captivating figure, and the audience was transfixed.

His speech that followed was rank with disdain and arrogance. He screamed, "Germany will no longer be the whipping boy of the developing world" For the first time, Hitler rallied the country and whipped up a fervor over the nation's difficulties. Tens of thousands bore witness, some out of rising pride and others out of sheer curiosity.

He called for mandatory military service by implementing a draft, defying the limits on military build-up Germany had agreed to after WWI. He was intent upon initiating extensive national infrastructure programs, including rebuilding highways, bridges, railways, and aqueducts. He promised to break the chains of economic hardship, while the rest of Europe was still in the midst of the Great Depression. He effectively captured the people's imagination.

In response to his announcement to rearm Germany (another direct violation of the Treaty of Versailles), he sought public approval to renounce the binds of the previous war and free the nation from the restrictions of this treaty. The world was on notice. European leaders were frantic.

A week later, Hitler announced the Nuremberg Laws, essentially stripping Jews of their civil rights as German citizens and legally separating them from society. Jews were also defined as a separate race as it related to the Law for Protection of German Blood and German Honor. Jews were summarily forbidden from serving in the military.

A swirl of nationalism followed in the days and weeks ahead. Nuremberg would be forever known as the epicenter of the Nazi movement.

Word of these developments hit Lisa exceptionally hard, especially since the rally was held in her hometown. It was all over the news and in the streets. What did this mean for her relationship with Johann? Would she ever even see him again, never mind would they, or could they, be together? Who was this enigmatic leader, and why was he so foreboding? Lisa took an immediate dislike to him. The rest of the family shared Lisa's abhorrence. Her father was the most outspoken critic, at least at home.

It immediately became apparent that citizens could not criticize Hitler in public, as there was mounting evidence that dissidents were disappearing. One of our neighbors was rumored to have been snatched out of his home in the middle of the night and shipped to a prison camp outside Munich called Dachau. He was a blue-collar worker and saw no good coming from this man. He said as much in public and apparently paid the price. The rising tension in our house was palpable.

Religions other than Judaism were under attack, as well. Priests and other clergy were also summarily rounded up and shipped out if they dared to open their mouths in disrespect. Others were just defrocked. Religion as an institution was under siege. Organizations of all kinds were threatened. My grandfather saw the folly in all of this and sensed the winds of war long before anything official occurred.

Inside the house, he screamed to anyone who would listen, "As a nation, we're still feeling the lingering effects of the last war, and with two military-aged sons and now a future son-in-law part of the military machine, the Bieswanger family on the whole wants nothing to do with this man."

Even after I was born, he also continued his disapproval of the unwanted new addition to the family, at least outwardly. But he couldn't keep himself from falling hard for this fair-haired, blue-eyed bundle of energy. I grew to be the favorite of his five grandchildren (at least I thought so).

His entire extended family ended up living under his roof for the duration of the war. Housing became a premium as war neared, forcing families to make the challenging decision to move in together. Life was certainly a trial, but since we had each other, we didn't know any better. Everyone we interacted with lived under similar circumstances.

CHAPTER FOUR

Hitler's Favorite City

My grandfather (Opa, as we called him) was a native of Nuremberg and was a bricklayer by trade. It was a good occupation, one that could sustain a family and put food on the table. He and my grandmother were in their mid-sixties by the time I was born. By 1938, the war machine started to ramp up when Germany annexed Austria. Then, in September of 1939, Germany invaded Poland. This was the beginning of our misery.

After Munich, Nuremberg is the second largest city in Bavaria. It's located in the northern end of the province and is the unofficial capital of the Franconian region, a hub of economic and cultural activity. It is distinguished by the medieval architecture of the Middle Ages. It is a walled city with a moat surrounding fortifications, garrisons, and stone towers, characteristically adorned with red-roofed buildings. At the northern edge of the old city (Altstadt) stands the Kaiserburg Castle, which dates back to the 14th century. It represented the power and importance of the Imperial City of the Holy Roman Empire.

The focal point of this vibrant city is the market, notably called the *Hauptmarket* or central square. This square is famous for its farmer's markets and seasonal celebrations. During the Middle Ages, the market attracted all the surrounding famers and artisans, where they sold their wares. This economic tradition continues to this day.

Seasonal festival events date back millennia, including the world-famous *Krist Kindl Markt* (Christ Child), held during Advent that attracts hundreds of thousands of tourists shopping during Christmas.

This square is also home to a number of ancient churches. They sit on opposing sides of the *platz*, looking down and keeping watch over its citizens. The most famous of these places of worship are the Schoener Brunnen with its majestic gilded fountain with tiers of figures near the front door, and the Gothic Frauenkirche, also built in the 14ᵗʰ century.

There was always plenty of work for a bricklayer in a city of brick buildings.

Because of its Middle-Ages era character and architecture, Nuremberg was also Hitler's favorite city. It is surmised that this was the reason Hitler chose to launch his Reign of Terror, masked as rebuilding the country, from this city. It was the cradle of the Nazi movement. At the time, this seemingly minor element would come to have a chilling impact on our lives, especially the longer the war raged on.

Although Opa was hardened by the rigors of his trade, he loved his city, too. He was the pillar of the family and the unofficial mayor of the neighborhood. He seemed like a giant to me, towering over our family like a shepherd over his flock. My earliest memories are of sitting on his lap and using my fingers to map all the deep cracks and crevices in his work-worn hands. He had hands the size of baseball mitts, yet despite their power, he held me tenderly. He was a true patriarch, finding a way to shelter and feed upward of ten to twelve people at any given time, despite food becoming increasingly scarce. To this day he remains my hero.

My grandmother (Oma) was born Francesca Mertz in the Czech Republic and was proud of her Gypsy legacy. She was a forgiving soul and couldn't help but love me from the outset. She spoke fondly about growing up in a large family and living in caravans at the close of the 19th century, always on the move throughout the region. Her family was made up of migrants traveling around Europe with indiscriminant borders, constantly looking for work, both legitimate as well as shady, should conditions demand it. Grifting (scamming the unsuspecting public) was a family tradition. The family caravan made its way to the eastern part of Germany, where the border lines were muted in the post-WWI rebuilding of Europe. This is where she met my grandfather. He was part of a big team building a wall brick by brick on the Donau (Danube) River outside of Budapest, Hungry.

My grandparents were very poor even before the war began, since our local economy was still reeling from the damage of the depression. We lived on the ground floor of a five-story walk-up brownstone just outside of the walled part of the city. It was in the low income section of the city. Each block consisted of twenty identical buildings, all attached on each side. Just down the street stood an ornate church built in the Baroque style, with a majestic spire and an attached brass cross standing one-hundred-and-eighty feet above us. It made me feel insignificant. One day I would conquer that feeling, as well as the church.

There were eleven of us--my two grandparents, my two aunts (Frieda and Wilma), my mother, my uncle's Jewish girlfriend Carla, who was in hiding with us and the five of us grandchildren/cousins (Lisa Lotte, Robert, Paul, Marichen, and me). We occupied two rooms with a small kitchen and no indoor plumbing. The three-seat outhouse in the back yard and communal water pump was shared by twenty families. While the quarters were tight, it made for a close-knit community. It was painful, but it was a shared, communal pain.

CHAPTER FIVE

Gypsy Roots

I remember the warmth of the kitchen stove as we sat around at night listening to Oma's stories about growing up as a Gypsy. Although diminutive in stature, to me she was larger than life. She made living life on the road seem glamorous. She was held in reverence within the family, as well as the community at large. She had a persona that belied her size. It would serve her well, standing up to the Nazis.

Her presence was almost transcendent, as if she was from another time and place What stood out most about her was that she made a living being a psychic reader. She utilized a mixed bag of tools to offer customers a glimpse into the past or future.

I remember her colorful tarot cards with ornately illustrated figures. They captivated me because of their flamboyant images and intrigue. She could read spent tea leaves and palms, as well. She had a way of making the supernatural seem normal. She could make us (and others) believe the unbelievable.

She had several appointments per week, mostly with women who would sit right at our kitchen table waiting to be transfixed. As word of her prowess got around the neighborhood, more and more customers came to Oma for guidance. Initially, her appointments were about the mundane questions of life or perhaps mystifying health issues. However, as the war waged on, these women wanted to know if their husbands or sons were alive or dead. She would read the cards with all of us grandchildren looking on from the shadows. She would tell them if they should continue to hope or if the situation was dire. Initially, these women would pay cash for her services. But as the war made currency scarce, monetary payment changed to a barter system. Homemade bread, chickens, eggs, and potatoes quickly became more valuable than hard currency.

Oma was an economic force that enabled her to subsidize my grandfather's income, which was meager at best, since he hardly worked in the early stages of the war. As an adult, I discovered the reason he didn't work as frequently as he would have liked was because he was not invited to join the bricklayer's union because he refused to join the Nazi Party. This meant little or no work in his trade. He was a man of principle, and his livelihood was constantly threatened by his political stance.

CHAPTER SIX

The Nazi Party

The Nazi Party, originally called the Worker's Party, was founded in 1919 as a direct result of the Treaty of Versailles following the end of WWI. In 1921, at the age of 32, Hitler became its leader. The party's platform was based on nationalistic principles and anti-Semitism. The Party framers felt the conditions under which this new Germany had to live were too onerous and stringent. The WWI treaty created new borders throughout Europe, leaving countries and regions altered beyond recognition. Some ethnic regions lost their identity, as well, leaving them feeling disenfranchised. Germany was left economically bereft as it was made to pay reparations it could never afford.

This was the fertile ground on which Hitler was able to sow national discontent.

Hitler wrote the book *Mein Kampfe,* which made him a millionaire. It was his manifesto and his blueprint outlining how Germany would once again rise to prominence. It was so popular, in fact, that from 1933-1945, a copy of his book was gifted to every newlywed couple in Germany by the Nazi propaganda machine. It was considered such a threat that in 1945, after the war ended, the book was summarily outlawed by the Allies.

The party gained significant popularity after his appointment as *Führer* in 1933. He outlawed all other parties and used fierce political and economic coercion to grow his party. He built the first concentration camp in

Dachau (outside Munich) in the same year, initially to imprison political adversaries.

It was no easy task keeping a roof over one's head under Nazi rule if you disagreed in any way with the party line. I clearly remember, starting in the early 1940s, a man, the *gauleiter*, who was both the landlord's agent and the district supervisor, would visit the apartment every month. I didn't like him because he was always disagreeable and cross.

He would open every conversation the same way:

"Josef, are you ready to join the Nazi Party?"

Every month, my grandfather would emphatically answer in the same way. "NO!"

The *gauleiter* would respond, "You have to join the Nazi Party or I cannot protect you any longer. If you don't join, I will be forced to evict you and your family. This apartment belongs to the city and only members of the party can live here."

Again, my grandfather would answer, "NO!"

Every month when the rent was due, this exchange would repeat, and every month the answer was the same. My grandfather, and by default the whole family, hated the Nazi Party. He saw the demonic propensities hiding among the good things on which most German people focused including the surge in nationalistic pride, the restoration of Germany's profile on the international stage that was on full display during the 1936 Olympics in Berlin, as well as all the infrastructure programs that made Germany a superpower once again.

Opa was not fooled, and he would not fold. In late 1942, on one of his visits, the rent collector declared, "Josef, if you are unwilling to join the party and you want your family to continue to stay in this apartment, you have to join the organization "Organisation TODT (OT)" You have left us no other choice!"

Orgainasion Todt was a civil and military, non-uniformed labor force. It did Hitler's bidding in his attempt to dominate Europe once occupied. If he agreed to join, my grandfather was to be shipped to the east coast of France to build submarine bunkers for the German navy. Seeing no other option and wanting to keep a roof over his family's head, he conceded and left a month later. He spent two years in France and was worked to the bone. It was the equivalent of slave labor. There was little food and the work conditions were appalling. In his absence, not only were we able to keep the apartment, but we received a small check every month, as well. As long as there were goods to buy, this income kept the family afloat.

As the war stormed on, consumer staples such as food items like bread, eggs, coffee, and meat, along with basic necessities such as clothing, shoes, toilet paper, and heating fuel became scarce due to the supply lines being cut, or it was commandeered for the troops. Local famers and merchants found a way to keep a black market economy humming, but hard currency was useless. Bartering became a way of sustenance and an economic necessity.

At the time he left, Opa was already 67 years old and given the physicality of his job, was in pretty good shape for his age. Although he returned in mid-1945, only two years later, he came home a broken, bitter, and much older man. He disclosed very little of his ordeal, but you could just tell it had been hell for him. Despite his sour disposition and resentful attitude, he remained my hero throughout my life. He did what he needed to do to keep a roof over our heads without compromising his values. He proved that not every German was a Nazi, nor could he be coerced to join the party. He was a man of conviction.

CHAPTER SEVEN

Wedding Bells

My father was more of a notion than a reality, having only visited a few times while on leave during my first five years. One of my earliest impressions of my father dates back to my parent's inevitable wedding day. It was in the summer of 1940. Papa was stationed in Berlin, still serving in the motor pool, and had been granted his first three-day pass. He used it as an opportunity to take a train back into town.

I remember a picture-perfect day. The sun was shining, a slight breeze stirred the air, and everyone around me seemed so happy. Apparently, his appearance had been a surprise. So was his suggestion to my mother upon his arrival on Friday night that they get married the very next day.

It was a warm sunny day, and everyone was wearing their Sunday best. There were so few occasions to dress up anymore, so I knew this was a special day. At noon, we all walked the two blocks to the local church as the bells played their melodic tune, ringing twelve times in succession. I, too, was dressed in a smart suit. At the ordained hour, I was coached to walk down the aisle of this majestic church as the pipe organ blared, carrying a delicate pillow with two rings pinned to it.

I was the ring bearer at my own parent's wedding.

My mother followed close behind me, carrying a small bouquet of roses. She looked radiant in her white brocade gown that was so long it hid her feet. Where she'd found it on such short notice has always been a mystery to me. My father stood at the front of the church, proudly wearing his military dress uniform. He looked quite handsome and debonair. At least, that is how my mother described him on occasions years later. She loved him even more on that day.

After a ceremony that, to a five-year-old boy, felt interminable, we walked in procession back to the house and through the ground floor corridor to the back yard. While we were at the church, the neighbors had taken it upon themselves to decorate the garden for a celebratory reception. Everyone cobbled together what little food they had so it actually resembled a feast. Everyone spontaneously coming together for this long-awaited union made it a day not soon forgotten. Then, just as quickly as he'd appeared, my father once again vanished from our lives the very next day.

CHAPTER EIGHT

The Winds of War Hit Home

I began to understand the impact of the war and what was going on around me soon after the wedding. My first thoughts always shifted to my grandmother, the strong matriarchal figure in our family. She was our moral compass. And her reputation as the town psychic and medium continued to grow.

I never really understood what she did or where her talents came from, but what I did see was hard to believe. However, my skepticism began to ebb with each and every session I witnessed. As the war intensified, more and more women came to the door, desperately asking about their loved ones and whether or not they were still alive.

The first real evidence of Oma's psychic abilities that I recall was at the end of 1941. By that time, my three uncles (my mother's two brothers, Paul and Hans, as well as my Aunt Wilma's husband, Fritz) were fighting in the war.

Utility services that all of us had taken for granted were beginning to fail throughout the city. Electricity was intermittent. Some days we had a few hours during the day and the night was dark, and then a day or two later we could turn the lights on for two or so hours at night and that was it. As time ticked by, entire days without electricity was becoming common. There was virtually no heat in the winter as heating fuel was rationed. The only warmth was supplied by the cooking stove that burned wood. We used to all gather in the kitchen to be warmed by the stove, share what little food we had, and listen to Oma's stories from her youth.

It was December 14, 1941, a day no one in our household would soon forget. The day was cold and raw. The wind visciously swirled around, finding its way into all the cracks in the building. At times, you could actually hear the wind whistle. I was six years old at the time, and my mother, her two sisters, my cousins, and my uncle's fiancée Carla were all huddled around the stove.

Oma held us captivated with one of her tales when all of a sudden, she clutched her chest and screamed, "Paul! Paul, NO!"

And then she fainted and fell over. She lay there completely unconscious on the floor. We thought it was just an act to help convince us of the validity of her narrative.

When she came to a few minutes later, she sat on the floor sobbing. Hysterically, she cried out, "Paul just died," and then sat staring out at nothing.

Then, as if someone flipped a switch, she regained her composure and continued, "I could hear the shot, and I could feel his pain. It was over in seconds."

We sat there in utter disbelief. The adults in the family tried to console her. We also did our best to dissuade her of this catastrophe and explained that she only had a "feeling," and reality could be totally different. Deep down, we kids just thought she was crazy.

Almost as if on cue, she turned silent. For days, she would speak to no one. She retreated into her own world. She looked hollow and beaten. She cried incessantly. Nothing we could say or do would console her. Each grandchild would take turns hugging her, thinking our affection would help her snap out of it. She just kept repeating the same words. "Paul is dead!"

About a week later, a telegram delivery boy knocked on our door. Oma answered the door and immediately slumped onto the floor. Opa heard the commotion and ran to the door. There stood the befuddled telegram boy handing the telegram to Opa as Oma wept at his feet.

He opened it and began to cry too.

It read:

"Private Paul Beiswanger died for the Fatherland on December 14th, 1941, at Weizima, Russia."

There was a collective gasp from the family as we all stood in the kitchen transfixed, listening to Opa.

Now we had the evidence that Oma truly had a gift.

Her son Paul, my uncle, died just as she had said, on the same day she'd fainted. In that moment, she'd made believers out of all of us, but she gained no satisfaction in being right.

After a few days, life went on as normal. Routine was the friend of the aggrieved. There still was a shroud of sadness hanging over the household. Regrettably, we were not alone in our sorrow. Many young men from our neighborhood were dying. Communally, the neighborhood shared a sense of dread, but it was something we all had to shoulder. Our visible anguish couldn't be any greater than our neighbors. A united front of solidarity was needed to muscle through. Without a word said, it was time to move on.

Oma started to come around, too. She found solace in the mundane tasks of the day.

Daily, we were reminded of our loss, as the enduring misery continued to surround us. Food remained scarce. Hunger was our closest companion, whether we wanted him near or not. Our days were spent scavenging for anything of value or to eat. Each grandchild would team up with an adult and head out for the day with a quest to bring something home.

A couple of weeks later, my grandmother received a letter from my uncle's best friend. It read as follows:

Dear Mrs. Beiswanger,

By now, I'm sure you have been informed that your son Paul died at Weizima, Russia on December 14th, 1941. I am deeply sorry and would like to tell you about his last moments. He and I had to walk across a bridge on patrol. Before we were over the water, we spotted what looked like a dead Russian soldier lying by the river's edge. Paul said we should climb down and check him out and make sure he was dead.

"He could have some intelligence on him that we could use as leverage."

As he approached the Russian, the soldier turned and fired a shot, hitting Paul in the chest. It was a trap. To his credit, Paul was able to get a shot off, killing the Russian. I climbed down off the bridge and found Paul still alive but gravely wounded. I spent a few minutes with him trying to stanch the bleeding. When I thought he was stable, I ran for help. About a mile down the road, I found the rear guard with a couple of medics. We ran back and Paul was put into an ambulance, where I joined him. I held his hand praying for the best. He died in the ambulance. His last words were, "Mother, Mother!" My comrades and I buried him in a Russian cemetery and I've enclosed a photo of his grave.

Sincerely,

Heinrich Roper

How does a mother get over such a loss? He died doing what he thought was best. How was he to know it was a trap?

It all felt so meaningless and abstract, especially to a young child. And to make matters worse, he'd been buried in Russia. Oma wanted him back, even just to hold him one more time. Once again, Oma retreated into silence. It was the hardest few months for all of us until she finally came around.

CHAPTER NINE

Air Raids as a Way of Life

In early 1942, as the war intensified, air raids became commonplace. It was something to which we grew accustomed, as strange as that may sound. It was a clarion call to action. Not every siren was followed by planes in the sky. And even if we did witness planes in formation, it didn't always lead to bombings, either. The officials in charge of our early warning system could not differentiate between a bombing raid and a flight platoon passing by on the way to another bombing sight deeper in Germany. The resulting reaction was somewhat subdued as we became immune to the warning of each siren blare.

Nonetheless, preparations were needed to minimize our risk. Every window in every building was covered up. The objective was for no light to be emitted and seen from the sky as a sign of life. As a result, no fresh air filtered through, either. Community leaders decided bomb shelters were needed. A room in the cellar of every building had to be converted and reinforced with columns and beams. Water, canned food, first aid supplies, clothing, blankets, and many other provisions had to be stored. Pass-through tunnels in-between building basements in the firewalls were dug out for alternative exits. For weeks, every able-bodied citizen was busy making these preparations.

The droning of airplane engines filled our ears shorty after dusk. Like clockwork at least once a night, the sirens would shriek and adults would summon us to the basement. We would sit by candlelight, shuddering to the sound of airplanes flying above and then suddenly cringing from the double cracks of the anti-aircraft artillery or flak. Fortunately, our city wasn't the target of the early raids. The planes were heading for more strategic targets, so they flew over us without dropping their bombs. More often than not, in thirty to forty-five minutes, the all-clear horn would sound and we could return to our beds. For us kids, sleep returned quickly, but the adults never quite recovered from each of the raids, and sleep was intermittent at best. They always looked exhausted on the mornings following an incursion, not knowing if they would live to see the sun come up.

As the war raged on, daytime air raids also increased in frequency. These were more exhilarating for us kids, but I'm sure more frightening for the adults. School was in session when the war first began. When the sirens would sound, the teacher would organize us and march us single file to the school's bomb shelter as if it were a fire drill. It was all so rehearsed. In 1942, the air raids became so frequent that school was suspended. This, of course, was met with utter joy by all the students. Schoolhouses were converted to makeshift infirmaries and temporary housing for those who'd been displaced by the bombs and were made homeless.

The more air raids and bombings that plagued the city, the more thrilling life became for an imaginative boy my age. To me, it was an adventure. Watching the sky fill with Allied planes was a sight to behold. The enemy planes converged upon each other in synchronized patterns and then dipped their wings, dropped altitude and discharged their ammunition. If we were able to sneak out successfully away from the watchful eye of a parent, a few friends and I would gather and watch as the inevitable dogfights ensued. We were always entertained by the theater in the sky as American fighter planes would engage the German Luftwaffe (airforce).

However, this peril was met with a much different response by my mother. As a result of her outward immunity to fear, she had always been my rock. At first, being a single mother gave her a sense of courage and sturdiness unmatched by her siblings. Despite this façade, she had an overt phobia of being buried alive. Therefore, we spent most nightly air raids standing just outside the basement doorway at the bottom of the stairs.

When the air raid sirens sounded, we would run from the apartment, out to the backyrad and then stop just short at the top of the stairs leading to the shelter. Dozens of neighbors from the upper floors would rush past us, each screaming, "Keep going, get in!"

And each time the two of us would just stand there, holding hands and looking up.

We could hear the roar of the airplane engines and would watch in awe as the planes crisscrossed and zigzagged through the sky. The beams of the spotlights from the Nazi defense forces would bounce off the clouds searching for the enemy. If a US or Allied bomber would get caught in a searchlight, all the other searchlight operators would converge their beams on that plane. The German soldiers on the ground controlling the flak guns would now concentrate their aim on the illuminated target while the enemy pilot, through evasive maneuvers such as dives, turns and barrel rolls, would desperately try to escape certain death. During really intense raids, the sky would be ablaze from planes exploding in the air, flares attached to bailing-out parachutes, explosions from the ground artillery or incendiary bombs that hit their mark across the city. The entire scene would always leave me mezmerized and breathless. I was too young to fully grasp the seriousness and danger of what was happening.

Daytime bombings were no less exciting. Standing in the doorway, we would watch the squadrons of planes fly over in various formations. Soon, the flak guns would engage and we could see the white cloud puffs of the exploding shells surrounding the squadrons of bombers. Every so often, there would be a sudden hole in one of the squadron formations as the flak would hit its target. I would strain my eyes to watch the plane spiral downward. It was particularly thrilling to watch for a parachute if the pilot and the crew were able to eject. Sometimes I would see the German air response appear, as well as the escort fighters. The ensuing dogfights were history in the making.

Our city was regularly bombed by English, French, and Russian planes by night and the Americans by day. After a while, I could tell the difference between each enemy plane just by the drone of the engine. That's how often the air sorties flew over our city.

More and more targets were hit, both industrial and civilian. Nuremberg was not a strategic city as far as factories, armaments, and supply lines were concerned. However, it was one of the epicenters for what life was like in Bavaria, which had a sense of *living in the moment*. Nuremberg embodied that ideal more than any other city in its day. We were a proud metropolis grounded in tradition, culture and the pursuit of happiness as way of life. The few citizens who still had radios and listened to the news reports fostered the belief that the Allies held fast to a strategic imperative that to win the war, they had to break the German spirit and bring the citizen population to its knees. And it was widely known that Nuremberg was Hitler's favorite city. So what better way to rub it in his face than to annihilate it? As it turned out, this strategy meant everything in turning the tide of the war.

CHAPTER TEN

Getting Through the Day

Life for civilians became perilously challenging. Most of the time, we were without water, gas, and electricity. Food had become increasingly scarce. Everything was rationed. Families would receive only so many grams of meat, butter, and bread per month. But even with the monthly allotment, it was never enough, especially for a family as large as ours. During the most trying times, the best of people would brightly shine through. Our neighbors looked out for us and vice versa. Everyone collectively shared what little they had. It was a sense of mutual misery, and to spread what little wealth was available brought a sliver of sheer joy to an otherwise wretched situation.

When the water was cut off, which happened a couple of times per week, my cousins and I would take an old milk can or two on a small pullcart and walk out to the countryside in search of any sign of water. If we were lucky, we would find a bomb crater partially filled with stagnating rainwater. The older kids would lower the younger kids (me) down into the trench so that we could scoop up the murky water. If it was really deep, we would make a human chain of three or four of us to reach the depths. Over time, we became quite adept in commandeering water from the most unlikely sources.

Hours later and with many miles behind us, we would arrive home with two or so cans of disgusting water. First, we would strain the water through an old sock to collect the sediment. Then we would light the stove with the kindling wood we'd also collected on the trail and then we'd boil the water. Once boiled, it was fit for human consumption and cooking. Bathing was a luxury no family could afford. Desperate times demanded extreme measures to survive.

Hunger was a shadow rarely shaken. Breakfast usually consisted of a piece of rye bread, a cup of skimmed milk, and, if lucky, an occasional egg. We usually skipped lunch, with the exception of an apple or pear on rare occasions. Dinner typically amounted to a bowl of watery soup, bread, and maybe a potato or two. Boy, did I get tired of potatoes! On most days, there wasn't enough food to satisfy one growing boy's appetite, keeping in mind that there were five children all living under one roof following the birth of my youngest cousin, Marichen. Candy or chocolate was out of the question. If available at all, sweet treats were reserved for a Christmas present.

More often than not, at six o'clock in the evening, my mother would demand that we all go to bed. "When you sleep, you don't feel the hunger," she would shout.

Christmas was like any other day, spent without a tree or presents. None of us children had toys, as they had all been put to more practical uses such as fuel for warmth.

As the war thundered on, the air raids intensified. More air raids also meant more time spent in the air raid shelter. Following every air raid, it was my mother's assignment to visit all the members of the family throughout the city to see if anybody's home had been hit and if any family member was wounded or dead. There were no telephones or any other methods to communicate with loved ones. And forget about public transportation. The street-car tracks had either been dug up to be used for armaments or were no longer viable, as they were buried under thousands of pounds of debris. My mother and I would walk all day from one side of the city to the other, searching for loved ones in various neighborhoods. Of course, this meant we would get caught out in the open during air raid warnings and subsequent bombing runs.

On one such occasion, the two of us were on the outskirts of town, maybe four miles from home. Out of nowhere it seemed, the skies filled with planes. We panicked. We were completely exposed! A kind, elderly gentleman called out from a ground level transom window, beckoning us to follow his voice. We ran as if our lives depended on it because, of course, they did. I practically ran out of my makeshift shoes.

We made it to the door of the building. As we turned and stood in the threshold, we watched a squadron of bombers approach from the west and release their bombs over the center of the city. The noise of the exploding bombs and the concussion of the ensuing flak guns was deafening. We both covered our ears. Flak guns are loud when they are fired, and even louder when they explode in the air, releasing thousands of small fuselage-piercing shrapnel that wounds or kills the pilots and/or gunners. Bombs were dropping within a few blocks of our location.

A heavy dust filled the air. It was almost as if we were frozen in time. Mesmerized, we didn't dare move a muscle.

My mother looked at me and yelled over the noise, "Hold my hand and don't let go, no matter what!" I could see the real, palpable fear in her eyes. It wouldn't be the last time she demanded I hold on for dear life.

Looking toward the city, the site was awesome! Five- and six-story buildings suddenly evaporated, collapsing floor on top of floor, only to bring into view other buildings which would then also disappear. The whole air raid was over in fifteen minutes. When the dust settled, all we saw were chimneys and the remnants of walls where houses had once stood. Where we had been now lay in ruins. Somehow, our temporary shelter had withstood the barrage.

After greeting the survivors coming up from the basement, we were met by the man who'd yelled at us from the window. We very graciously hugged this stranger and thanked him profusely for saving our lives. Later in the week, we returned and brought him two eggs and a potato for being so kind.

We continued our journey undeterred, climbing over rubble and staying out of the way of screaming women and children covered in soot as sirens wailed and rescue workers helped people climb out of cellars, lucky to be alive. Although their lives had been narrowly spared, they were devastated for having lost what little they had. They were facing an uncertain future of hunger and homelessness. I was maturing quickly and had learned to appreciate my home and the family I still had. Every time I returned from one of these journeys, I felt blessed that I still had all of my meager possessions.

Although my father was granted very few weekend passes, during the early years of the war, he was stationed in Berlin, close enough for us to visit. Early in the war, my mother and I managed to take three trips by train early to spend some time with him. This was always exciting for me, not only because of the train ride, but also because we stayed on the army base. I watched the hectic pace of military life coupled with the endless traffic of interesting military equipment. Every day, soldiers marched stoically in front of us. At times, nationalistic or marching type music played throughout the base on aluminum speakers hung from poles. It was meant to inspire the soldiers' patriotic spirit.

Traveling to visit my father was not without its perils. It was quite common for the train to immediately grind to a halt at hearing the air raid sirens sound. The brakes would squeal at a shrill pitch and the train would come to an abrupt stop. The passengers were told to jump off and run for the woods.

On our last trip, I vividly remember the train grinding to a halt. My mother looked at me and screamed above the sirens, "Hold on to my hand tightly. Never let go, and run as fast as you can. If I fall and cannot continue, I need you to keep running and find another adult to shelter with."

I did as I was told. We would heed the warnings, and while holding hands, we would sprint for any type of cover. We would huddle with strangers behind rock outcroppings, clinging to each other for warmth or out of fear. Within minutes, dive bombers and machine gunners would appear over our heads, strafing the trains and trying to take out the front locomotive. Most of the trains carried military equipment, and several flat cars were equipped with guard cannons and flak guns. Once under attack, the tarps would be pulled off the train cars and the flak gunners would take aim. It was loud and intolerable. Fortunately, the attacks were never that successful. We were never left stranded, and after some delay, the train

would move on. By the middle of 1944, conditions became so precarious that all travel by train stopped.

CHAPTER ELEVEN

The Final Solution Uncovered

As the war fumed, I became more aware of the political climate. Conversations were subdued and held in closed quarters. People looked worried, constantly watching over their shoulders. Rumors of concentration camps and death camps made the rounds. People talked of neighbors and friends disappearing. Nighttime raids by the Gestapo and the SS (Schutzstaffel) were rampant.

The Gestapo had the authority to investigate cases of treason, espionage, sabotage and criminal attacks on the Nazi Party and Germany. The basic **Gestapo** law passed by the government in 1936 gave the **Gestapo** carte blanche to operate without judicial review. In effect, the Gestapo was above the law.

The SS started out as a small paramilitary group formed to protect Hitler and other Nazi officials. Over time it became the unit tasked with carrying out the extermination of all enemies of the state including Jews, scholars, clerics, gypsies, homosexuals and the mentally ill. Ulitmatley, the SS ran the concentration camps.

For me, this was the first time I became personally exposed to the evil workings the Nazi party.

I have vivid memories imprinted from the second grade. School wasn't interrupted until I was about to enter third grade, when the war became so intense that it was deemed unsafe to attend. Given that air raids were less common in the morning, we had to leave early for school, arriving even before the teachers. Once assembled together, we were just like ordinary students, with little or no supervision, always up to mischief. We would cause mayhem in the classroom while one student would be tasked with monitoring for an approaching adult. He or she would stay in the hallway and when the lookout saw the teacher approach, they would run in yelling, "The teacher is coming!" We would then scramble to our seats, putting on a convincing act of innocence.

When the teacher entered, the lookout would yell "Achtung (attention)!" We would jump to our feet and say, "Guten Morgen, Herr Lehrer," which meant, "Good morning, Mr. Teacher." One morning, as we entered the classroom, we noticed a man wearing a black leather coat and knee high boots. He emminated a dark, foreboding attitude and sat in one of the seats in the back. Under his trenchcoat he wore a crisp black uniform prominently displaying an armband with a swastika. He looked quite intimidating. Although its power was somewhat incomprehensible, the swastika was beginning to slowly creep into our young, impressionable minds. We had no idea why this man was there, but he scared the life out of us.

On this occasion, when our teacher entered, we went through our usual routine. We instinctively knew to be on our best behavior. As we settled down, the man got up and walked to the front. With obvious disdain, he ignored the teacher and started to address us in a fatherly tone. He told us about the goodness of our Führer (leader) Adolf Hitler, and how as good children of the Fatherland, we needed to show our respect for Hitler and the Third Reich.

He said, "From now on, children, we will no longer say good morning to Mr. Teacher, but we are to rise to our feet, raise our right hand and shout, 'Heil Hitler!'"

As if on cue, he snapped to attention, raised his right arm and shouted, "Heil Hitler!" We jumped to our feet and did as he commanded. He did it again, this time with more force. Again, we followed his lead, some with more enthusiasm than others. We then had to do the same as he left the room, mimicking his every move.

We were stunned. Silence hung in the air. The teacher looked as shocked and apprehensive as the rest of us. Slowly, the teacher got up, checked the hallway, and then looked back at us with wide, serious eyes as he said in a low but firm voice, "You will never do as this man told you. You will continue to say, 'Good morning, Herr Lehrer.'" And then he went on about his lesson plan for the day. Nothing more was mentioned. Slowly, the air came back into the room.

One week later, we walked into school to find a new teacher. He immediately addressed us in a serious tone and said, "Every morning when I walk into the room, you will stand. I will say, 'Good morning students,' and you will raise your right hand and say, 'Heil Hitler!' at least three times."

We understood as much as our young minds could. We complied consistently as instructed and never misbe-haved. Nobody ever heard from the original teacher again.

Throughout the war, I distinctly remember seeing people in our neighborhood and throughout the city wear-ing the Star of David patch on their clothing. My uncle Paul's fiancée Carla, although not practicing, had Jewish ancestors. As a precaution, from the onset of the war and even after my uncle died, she stayed with us and very rarely left the house. It didn't seem unusual to me, since we stayed indoors most of the time, anyway. Religion was also not discussed much in the family, so of course the idea of being a Jew was beyond what my youthful innocence could comprehend. I didn't understand such hatred.

This underlying fear of persecution for any misstep made everyone in the family quite apprehensive. The SS was never far from our thoughts. Even our family began to talk in hushed tones behind closed doors as if the walls were surely listening. Not long after the teacher debacle, we had our own interaction with this dark force. It was an especially harsh winter, and darkness collected us earlier each day. We had just finished our meager dinner. Our nightly ritual was to sit around the stove in the kitchen to stay warm while we talked. On this particular night, we were all there--my grandparents, my mother, my two aunts, my uncle's fiancée Carla, and all of us cousins.

Oma was delighting us once again with her gypsy tales. She was comically explaining what it was like to live in a caravan with such a large group and to move around from place to place. There was a short lull in the conversation, when all of a sudden our lighthearted mood was interrupted by the squawking of sirens. We had heard this sound many times before, but this time it felt different. Now, the sirens were approaching our front door, followed by the screeching of tires, car doors slamming and boots on the sidewalk stomping down the stairway hall. Suddenly, there was a violent knock at our door. It sounded ominous, like the butt of a rifle trying to break down the door.

We all stiffened as the air was sucked from the room. My grandmother, all of five feet tall, wearing a shabby house dress with her hair in a babushka, got up from the table. To me at that moment, she looked like a giant. Somehow, I found myself standing next to her as she stood up. I held her hand as she walked to the door, wondering who protected whom. She opened the door.

Looming large above us were three SS officers wearing long, dark leather trenchcoats, stiff hats, and matching leather gloves.

The officer in the middle demanded, "Where is the Jew?"

Oma indignantly and confidently replied, "What Jew?"

In an instant and without one word uttered, I watched as a rifle butt rose up and hit my grandmother square in the middle of her forehead. She stood there like a zombie before crumpling to the floor. She'd been knocked unconscious! I knelt beside her crying and screaming her name. The three SS soldiers stepped over Oma and me and went to the kitchen.

The same soldier screamed, "Which one of you is the Jew?"

Everyone froze. No one dared move or answer.

The man then continued yelling "Okay, you will all be arrested. Get up and come with me!"

As two of the SS officers walked toward the family to apprehend them, Carla stood up and declared, "I am the Jew." I still didn't know what a Jew was, but apparently it made these men stiffen with anger.

In seconds, two of the three leather clad robots dragged her out of the apartment screaming and writhing like a wounded animal. I've never heard a shriek like that before or since.

We all stood there dumbfounded, not knowing what to do or even what to say. We hardly discussed it in the days that followed. There was this unspoken feeling that we weren't allowed to discuss it. Over time, we all realized life continues.

As time went on, this incident haunted my dreams. What had Carla done wrong? What had caused this intrusion? In my childish innocence, I could not grasp this harsh treatment of another human being, especially one whom I loved so much.

I began to ponder similar incidents I'd witnessed, such as the disappearance of neighbors, friends, our parish priest, and our teacher. They were all considered *enemies of the state*. I began to understand my grandfather's bravery by abstaining from this political movement. Maybe he was wiser than I had thought. He certainly earned my respect. He never did join the Nazi Party. He stood firm in his beliefs despite the vicious threats to him and his family. What kind of man had the guts to stand up to these demons, especially in light of the deadly alternatives? He was even willing to harbor a Jew despite the likelihood of suffering harrowing consequences.

It wasn't until the war was over that we were confronted by the raw truth.

We were collectively shocked and appalled by the plan to exterminate the Jewish population, the infirmed, the mentally ill, the clergy, and any and all political opponents who defied the regime. These atrocities were too horrific to believe. How was our government capable of such carnage? The shame and disbelief was written on the faces of every adult I encountered. It was as if they were each individually shouldering this burden for the entire country.

The American and Allied military were also in shock with what they found when they liberated these camps in 1945. The evidence of mass extinction was hard to cover up. Pictures were released for the world to see.

Once the evidence of the crimes against humanity committed at these concentration camps was revealed, President Truman ordered the gates to the camps opened and forced the local citizens of these towns and surrounding areas to tour the camps and see firsthand for themselves what was being perpetrated right in their own back yards.

When they walked through the gates, they were greeted by the same propaganda that had greeted each prisoner,

"Arbeit macht Frei (Work makes freedom)!"

The irony was not lost on anyone after what they were made to witness.

The president's goal was threefold: to expose ordinary German citizens to the atrocity which had been carried out by their government, to ensure it would never be forgotten, and to guarantee that it would never happen again. He reasoned that without understanding the extent of the problem, the German population could not be a part of the solution.

As for Carla, for several years we didn't know what had happened to her. In quiet, hushed family discussions, we did ponder her fate. In the summer of 1947, she suddenly showed up without notice, walked into the apartment and visited my grandparents.

She revealed that she'd been sent to the Dachau concentration camp outside of Munich and was held there for over a year in appalling conditions. She recounted that during that time, she witnessed prisoners getting shipped to other camps, in particular Auschwitz. Many prisoners died from disease and mass execution at the camp. She'd been fearful she would be shipped out, as well. However, she escaped further incarceration when she was able to prove that one of her grandfathers was not Jewish. She confessed that if not for the sanctuary she'd received in my grandparents' home and the delay of being sent to the camps, she never would have survived a longer detainment under such deplorable conditions. By the time she finally returned to visit us, she actually appeared quite healthy.

CHAPTER TWELVE

The Chosen City

As the war went on, life got even tougher. The battle lines started to shift closer to home. At the beginning of the war, the fighting was esoteric because it was occurring on foreign fronts. As the Allies began their successful attacks, the incursions came closer and closer to home.

Rumors ran throughout our ghetto of an unsuccessful attempt to assassinate Hitler. Although it took some time to filter throughout the country, it was reported that on July 20, 1944, Claus von Stauffenberg and other conspirators attempted to kill Adolf Hitler inside his Wolf's Lair field headquarters near Rastenburg, East Prussia. The name Operation Valkyrie, originally referring to part of the conspiracy, became associated with the entire event. Someone in Hitler's inner circle got close to him and detonated a bomb, but it only wounded him slightly.

The goal was to wrest control of the military and, in turn, the government, and then immediately begin negotiations with the Allies to end the war.

For a moment, there was at least a glimmer of hope for those of us who didn't support him and wanted this war to be over, but it was quickly dashed. The prevailing thought, however, was that this was a sign of an insurrection in his leadership circle. One could only continue to pray.

By the late summer of 1944, we had gotten used to the air raids, the bombings, and the conflicting political climate, but it was hard to get used to the constant hunger. Collectively, we were all walking skeletons. The women in the family did the best they could to put food on the table. If it was a good summer growing season, there was a slight uptick in the availability of vegetables and hence the farmers' ability to barter. Occasionally, my mother would gather up some of the family heirlooms she still had left and strike out into the countryside to trade with farmers for potatoes, beans, cucumbers, bread, butter, eggs, or meat. She would usually come home exhausted with little to show for her meager assets, but if she was lucky that day, she would have just enough to sustain us for a few days. The problem was that the farmers, besides being on rations themselves, had to meet food quotas for the military and could keep very little food for themselves.

Although having just turned nine, I knew I needed to do more to help out in this endeavor. I had an idea. I knew that if successful, I would be the toast of the family and maybe even the neighborhood, for this particular act required bravery--or stupidity, depending on to whom you spoke. I had my eye on the ornately decorated bronze cross sitting atop the steeple of our local church. The steeple itself stretched approximately 150 feet into the air. The cross itself looked as if it was maybe four-to-five feet tall and three feet across. I knew I could trade it for at least a week's worth of food, maybe more. The challenge was getting up there and then down again, securing it safely, especially since it was most likely bigger than me.

I had been in and out of that church many times. I knew my way around the building well. I believed I had a plan.

One morning in late November, I snuck in the back door during a sparsely attended mass. I quietly made my way up the back stairs to the bell tower. I climbed out of the tower onto the spine of the roof over the body of the church. I just had to traverse across maybe 200 feet to the steeple. I refused to look down as I began my journey. As I got to the base of the steeple, people below started to take notice of me. A crowd soon gathered as they all stood there pointing up at me. Mass had just ended, too, so even more of the neighborhood joined the spectacle. Being so high, I was fairly unrecognizable, and this added to the mystery for the crowd below. Finally reaching the base of the cross, I still had 30 feet to conquer. The pole the cross sat on was thick enough for me to shimmy up. Once I reached my destination, I held on for dear life as I rocked back and forth, trying to pry the cross loose. After about five minutes, I felt it release. It was now mine.

But now what? As it turned out, it was slightly bigger than me and weighed less than I'd anticipated. Yet I still had to get down, only this time I had this awkward cross to carry. I carefully tucked it under my arm, stuck the arm inside my belt and shimmied back down. As I reached the roof, I heard cheering from below as now I had a growing fan base. But the noise also brought the priest out, who quickly notified the police. I needed to get off the roof and fast. The challenge of getting away with my prize trumped the fear of falling, but I found another way out through a transom window in the tower which I managed to pry open. This led to a spiral staircase in the spire. I disappeared in a blink.

Later that week, my mother was able to barter it for two dozen eggs, a large bag of potatoes, and some butter.

Christmas of 1944 uneventfully came and went. Due to shortages in everything, once again there was no tree, no toys, and no gifts. One would think this would be a hardship for five children all under the age of twelve, but by this time we had all grown immune to the inconveniences of life. Food and water were our most desired gifts.

My impression was that people everywhere were growing weary of the war, the bombings, the hunger and the loss of loved ones. I heard people growing increasingly afraid of what might happen in the very near future should Germany fall. We knew it was just a matter of time.

The wireless carried news of the Allied invasion from the west, the north, and the east. We were unsure if we were to be invaded by the French, the English, the Americans, the Russians, or all of them at once. It didn't take long before stories spread about the harsh treatment being doled out by the Russians as they marched in from the east. There were horrific accounts of women being raped or killed and homes being pillaged. It became abuntantly clear from these tales that no one wanted to see a Russian uniform. Gossip circled about mass executions of German POWs at the hands of the Russians, as well as anyone even remotely suspected of conspiring with or harboring German soldiers. No one was sure which was worse--continuing the war we knew or facing the unknown that lay ahead.

The Americans were dropping leaflets written in German telling people that the war would be over soon, and no citizen should offer any resistance or harbor any German soldiers. Anyone found guilty of aiding and abetting German soldiers would be considered an enemy combatant, and it could prove fatal. The message was clear-- don't help the retreating German army.

In spite of this shred of good news, the bombing raids went on unimpeded day and night. Most industrial targets in every big city had already been destroyed by this point. Factories were burned out and in ruins. Many houses, apartments, and churches, especially around the outlying industrial complexes, were destroyed. My own city was in ruins to the point where you couldn't tell one city street from the next. Entire neighborhoods were gone.

But things could always get worse, and they were about to, in a devastating way. I'll never forget the date. It was January 2, 1945. Since Christmas, things had been relatively quiet. It was a frigid but crystal-clear day. Blue skies as far as one could see. The quiet, clear day caused a misplaced sense of complacency. We woke at sunrise and plans were discussed and developed about going to scavenge again. Most of our activities had been suspended, given that the weather since New Year's Day had been brutally cold. Our warm-weather clothes were threadbare and due to the chilly temperatures, no one was really motivated to leave the warmth of the kitchen.

At about 10 o'clock, as we gathered together to stay warm, we heard a distant rumbling in the sky to the northwest. No early warning sirens went off, since by that time most wires and cables had been cut beyond repair. We just sat there staring at each other as foreboding washed over us. We knew this sound was different, louder. Over the years of daily bombardment, I had developed a keen ear for airplane engines. I could distinguish between the different types of airplanes just by the whirl of their engines, which usually meant I could tell whether or not we were in danger. The rumbling I heard on this particular morning sent chills down my spine and paralyzed me with fear.

I could sense that this was not going to be an ordinary bombing run. The hair on the back of my neck sizzled with fear. Something was different. The sheer cacophony and synchronization of the engines was louder than anything we'd ever heard before. Everything around us was beginning to vibrate as the droning intensified and the planes drew near. Teacups and plates fell from the cupboard.

I could hear the defensive flak cannons on the outskirts of Nuremberg go into action, trying to knock these planes out of the sky. Fear turned into action as people throughout our building started to scramble down the stairs to the basement. My mother and I sprinted to the back door that went out to a courtyard, looking west over the church, which was now missing a cross. As fleeing neighbors ran past us, they yelled, "Get to the basement!"

As before, Mama refused. We stood at the top of the stairs, craning our necks to the sky. Then our neighbors took to begging. Something was different this time, they explained. We were all alone in seconds.

I stood next to Mama, holding her hand, in total awe of the sight unfolding before my eyes. There were so many planes that they completely blanketed the sky and blocked out the sun. Squadron after squadron of bombers appeared over the roof of the church. The sky literally darkened. There must have been hundreds or even thousands of planes, my young mind thought, as the roar of the engines and the endless report of flak totally overwhelmed my senses.

Just as I thought we were witnessing Armageddon, all hell broke loose. Within minutes, hundreds and hundreds of planes had passed over our house and appeared now to be hovering atop the center of the city.

All at once, they released their bombs. Synchronized carpet bombing, I thought.

All around me, I could hear the high pitches and whistles of falling bombs with subsequent deafening explosions. We closed our eyes, put our hands over our ears, and ducked from time to time, as if we were the targets. The ground shook and dust filled the air. It was so loud you couldn't hear anying. Time stood still. The apocalypse had arrived.

Mama yelled to me, "The bomb whistle you hear won't hurt you!"

I guess she said this more to calm herself than me. Suddenly, right in the middle of all the chaos, I heard a rushing, whizzing sound. It sounded more like water hissing through a garden hose than the shriek of a whistle. In the blink of an eye came an unbelievably loud explosion. Everything shook violently! We were hit with a combination of flying debris, thick dust, and shattered glass as the two of us were thrust down the open stairway in the back yard to the basement. We must have fallen ten or twelve steps. I landed on top of a man who, in a panic, was trying to run up the stairs. My mother fell on top of me. The air in my lungs was dislodged from the fall and I could barely breathe.

Screams of, "We were hit, get out," snapped us out of shock and back to reality.

In the aftermath, we were literally lifted up, almost like celebratory heroes, and carried up the stairs and out the door by the hysterical mob of people who appeared to be afraid of being buried alive just like my mother had been. I found myself suddenly standing on the sidewalk in the garden, blinking through dust and debris, attempting to catch my breath. All around me, people were running and screaming. Many were bleeding, and all were crying.

We followed the crowd and left the back garden toward the front of the building. When my eyes adjusted and the smoke cleared, I looked across our street at the opposing apartment building. Where there used to be the facade of a five-story sandstone complex, a life-sized open-face dollhouse now stood. The entire front wall of the building had collapsed straight down to the curb. On each and every floor, all of the rooms were left completely intact and practically undisturbed. Tables, chairs, and lamps stood in place. Flowers still sat in ornate vases on the tabletops and pictures still hung neatly on the walls. A husband and wife sitting at their dining room table looked down at us in complete shock, he still holding his newspaper, she in her nightgown. They were staring down at us in complete shock. Why hadn't they fled for the shelters?

I turned to look up at our building and saw the evidence of what had transpired. The smoke was just clearing and the sun made me squint. A huge, one-ton bomb had pierced the roof of our house, leaving a big hole. Once the bomb hit our roof, it detonated the time-delay fuse, initally leaving our home still virtually unscathed. As the bomb continued its flight, it hit the building across the street, nailing it between the first and second floor and exploding on impact.

While barely breaking a glass on the neighbor's third floor dining room table, the explosion collapsed the front wall of the building from top to bottom. You could see into every apartment as if privacy never existed.

The subsequent force of the blast from the explosion and the resulting air pressure blew back across the street and through our building from front to back, resulting in the shattering of all the windows and doors of not only our building but also the entire city block. Anything not nailed down, such as furniture, dishes, and decorations, had been blown out the back of our house.

As I stood in shock and utter disbelief, I noticed a small fire starting way up in the eaves of the newly created doll house. Within a few minutes the entire roof was ablaze. As if someone had flipped a switch, frantic action ensued as panicking neighbors labored to free a passage to the basement of the burning building. As the occupants upstairs realized the impending danger, they climbed down a makeshift ladder someone had hoisted up and out of the rubble. Everyone was screaming, all obviously still dazed. The man upstairs still had his newspaper with him as he descended. I stood on the sidewalk and watched the building burn to the ground in less than ten minutes. But at least everyone got out safely.

Though it felt more like days, the bombing raid lasted less than thirty minutes. Close to 600 British planes unleashed over 6,000 high explosive bombs and more than 1,000,000 incendiary devices. When it was over, many buildings in our ghetto had been devastated beyond repair and the city as a whole was destroyed. I later learned that 80% to 90% of the city structures had been destroyed or badly damaged. It was estimated that 1,800 citizens had perished, 3,000 were injured, and more than 100,000 Nuremberg residents, including old men, women, and children were left homeless.

Only the city Wurzburg suffered more damage than Nuremberg in the state of Bavaria.

After the shelling, the air was thick with dust and ash that covered everything. We had to breathe through damp towels or wet handkerchiefs to filter the air. A cough into a handkerchief colored it black. Nuremberg was an inferno. At night, the entire city was aglow. It had an eerie red hue and, coupled with the black clouds of smoke and ash, it all seemed like hell on earth. At least that's what I imagined hell would look like.

To my astonishment, Nuremberg burned and smoldered for weeks. Despite it being the middle of January, trees and flowers started to blossom from the heat. If you closed your eyes and didn't know any better, you might have thought it was summer. And forget about snow. We didn't see a flake again until the following winter.

We spent the first few days sifting through rubble and salvaging what we could. We used lumber to board up the windows. Furniture was set upright, dusted off, and put back in place. Whatever dishware that hadn't shattered was reclaimed. The effort we five kids put forth was to rid the rooms of dust and bombing residue. Food, always at the center of our universe, became an afterthought. We were just too busy and exhausted to think about eating.

Four days after the raid, with the threat finally over, my mother and I went out on our usual mission to check on our relatives. Our first priority was to get to my paternal grandmother's house. She lived about four miles away on the other side of the city, which meant that we had to pass through some of the most devastated areas. We started at 8 o'clock in the morning, and from our first steps, the going was tough. Almost every street was blocked. We had to climb over mountains of rubble, through back yards, over makeshift passageways, and around piles of smoldering embers. Everywhere you looked, people were still digging, either looking for trapped survivors, recovering bodies or rummaging for personal items.

A journey that should have taken two hours took us close to six. As we approached the block where my grandmother lived, we saw that the entrance was completely blocked. Her immediate neighborhood consisted of three long parallel blocks totaling 120 four-story brown stone buildings. The three streets intersected one connecting cross street.

In the very middle of the second block, the city had built a huge concrete bunker to serve as a community air raid shelter. Ironically, people in the neighborhood did not like to use it. They felt it was a target and hence was unsafe. As we neared the block from the main road, we were halted by a pile of rubble so tall that it seemed to reach beyond the sky.

My mother told me to climb to the top to see what lay on the other side. Like the little scamp that I was, I quickly scaled the pile, probably thirty to forty feet in height. From that vantage point, I could see that most of the three-block ghetto was in ruins. Only three buildings in line with the front of the bunker and the bunker itself were still standing. There was no sidewalk or passageway to get in or out anywhere. Lingering, smoldering fires were dispersed throughout. It appeared that the entire neighborhood was working with one purpose. The flurry of activity indicated they were digging for survivors.

I helped my mother up and over the pile and we worked our way to my grandmother's house, which, we realized as we got closer, was one of the three houses still standing out of more than one hundred. What a relief!

My mother was ecstatic!

As we got close to her house, we saw a 40-foot by 50-foot square cleared of debris. Inside that square were about 20 to 30 bodies, covered in sheets, lying side by side. Surviving family members and neighbors had not been able to dispose of these bodies as of yet. I hastily realized that there was no easy way to carry a body out, since there was no exit and not enough manpower to carry body after body over the rubble pile.

Within the cleared area, I saw a little blonde girl, maybe three or four years old, sitting near two bodies who were obviously her parents. Between sobs and begging her parents to get up, she played with a stuffed toy. Even as young as I was, this wasn't the first time the idea of death and loss impacted me, but the depth of the devastation and suffering this girl displayed really hit me. And it hit me hard! The memory of that little girl crying into her doll will never leave me.

We found my grandmother still alive but obviously in a state of shock. She sat us down in her living room and told us about her terrifying ordeal as the bombs exploded all around her. Her house shook, and as she was making her way to the shelter, she got thrown to the ground and must have passed out. Everything in the apartment had been strewn about the floor by the time she awoke. Luckily, they had opened all the windows so they wouldn't be broken by the blowback from the percussion, but there was dirt and dust everywhere. She showed us the six-inch crack in the middle of the living room, through which the cold air of winter was constantly blowing in. She told us about the rescue efforts to find and dig up those who were still buried. Some came out alive, but some were still down there.

Occasionally, the survivors could be heard banging on pipes. Additional efforts were immediately commandeered and deployed to where they thought the noise was coming from. The lucky ones were rescued and brought out blinking against the sun they hadn't seen in days. Some were miraculously unhurt, while others had devastating injuries. Unfortunately for some, time ran out and the banging stopped.

The sound was about to drive Grandmother mad when we showed up. Rescue efforts were impeded by a lack of manpower and tools. My mother and I were yet strong enough to jettison this 65-year-old woman up and over the piles of rubble that stretched for blocks. Within a few hours, we had shepherded her back to our house and to safety.

I remember coming home late that night exhausted and starving. The rest of my family, awakened from their nightmares by the sight of our grandmother, launched into celebration. I hadn't eaten all day, but my hunger was slightly placated by the joyous atmosphere around me.

However, hunger can only be ignored for so long. Mama set about to make soup. The sound of lids clanging on pots and bowls being distributed whet our appetites. Unfortunately, once again, it was just watered-down soup with a few bits of bread that didn't help to alleviate the sharp pangs in any substantial way.

In the following days, with what little strength we had left, we managed to visit the rest of the relatives around town and miraculously found that nobody had died as the result of the bombings. As fate would have it, no one in our extended family lived in the heart of the city, which had sustained the lion's share of the damage and had suffered the most loss of life.

The weeks that followed amazed me. People were digging everywhere I looked. Temporary shelters made of plywood and bomb debris popped up throughout the city. People donated rescued pieces of furniture, and neighbors helped neighbors. The infrastructure of an advanced society ceased to exist. There was no water or electricity citywide. Having accomplished their goal of neutralizing and immobilizing Hitler's favorite city, the Allied bombing raids were over. A quiet sense of the inevitable started to creep over us like a warm blanket. It was even more obvious that the war was coming to a close! Some of the internal strife abated, as well. Civilians were no longer hassled by the Nazi party bosses, and after a few weeks, life slowly seemed to go back to some degree of normalcy.

CHAPTER THIRTEEN

Closing in on the End

We knew of a few neighbors who had illegal radio sets, and the underground news network was hard at work spreading stories about the Allied invasion that had begun at Normandy the spring before. Reports continued to circulate that it would only be a matter of time before Hitler would be defeated and the war would come to an end.

We prayed daily for the safe return of my dad, as well as for all the other relatives and friends still fighting in the war. We hadn't had a letter from Papa in over a year, and did not know where he was. We believed he might still be up near Berlin, where a lot of the heavy battles were being fought. We also prayed that we would fall into the hands of the Americans and not be captured by the French, English, or especially the Russians.

The unforgiving winter of 1945 slowly turned into the spring of 1945. As far as the fighting was concerned, things were relatively quiet. There were a few more bombing raids during the winter but nothing remotely close to what had happened in January. On April 11, 1945 the bombing suddenly stopped, and people went about their daily chores of cleaning up the streets and rummaging through the rubble. The war wasn't over, but we had the sense that the worst was behind us, or so we hoped.

The lingering harshness of being on the losing side of the war was evident all around us. There was still very little food. The stores were empty. When word got around that a butcher, a baker, or a market had a fresh supply of goods, people would flock to the location and stand in line for hours, often in vain. By the time they got to the front of the line, there would either be very little to buy, or the store would be out of everything. Subsequently, it would close again. We would venture out into the countryside to scavenge for anything edible, including potatoes, berries, and leafy greens. Oftentimes, we returned emptyhanded.

Every so often, a farm animal would die. The animal, be it a cow or horse, would then be dragged into town and brought to the butcher. Rumors of fresh meat would send the whole town into a frenzy. Horse meat was never considered a staple, but when desperation is your everyday state, horse meat is like manna from the gods! The women were very adept at making the inedible into a banquet, even if it was a harsh cut of meat or just the remnants of organs. You received your share based on how fast you could get to the butcher. I remember one time wating in a long line at the butcher with my mother. After a few patient hours, she was given a big package, no questions asked. When we got home, she dropped it on the table in front of everyone. As she unwrapped it, our eyes bugged out when we found ourselves staring at huge cow tongue. As unappealing as it looked, three hours later we enjoyed one of the best gourmet meals of the war. I don't know what my grandmother did, but after one bite we quickly forgot what we were eating, it was that delicious (or we were that hungry).

Everybody was pumping their neighbors for the latest on the war. Reports were flooded with details about what the French and the Russian soldiers were doing to the German civilians as they pushed through Germany. Mothers and daughters were being raped, sometimes in front of their family. Rape and savage beatings were tools used to punish the citizens for fostering an environment that had let a maniac like Hitler rise to power. We heard that hundreds of towns and cities were surrendering. Homes were being ransacked, with soldiers looking to take home anything of value. Only the Americans were believed to be civil. Of course, everybody hoped the U.S. GIs would get to our town first.

In late March, leaflets in German written by the Allies once again fluttered down from planes all over the city, informing us that the Americans would soon enter the area near Nuremburg and street fighting was to be expected. The flyer said that the civilian population would not be considered as hostiles as long as they behaved as prescribed. Everyone was instructed to stay indoors. Doors and windows were to be barricaded. Anyone seen in the streets or at the windows would be considered enemy combatants or partisans and would be fired upon. Our shortlived lull in the war was about to end, and our lives would again be in peril. We waited, sitting on pins and needles, anxious for what would transpire next. The battle of Nuremburg was about to ensue.

News was filtering in through the underground wire networks. We had heard that the German High Command had ordered the unconditional defense of all cities. The local leadership of the Third Reich decided to make a last-ditch effort to stem the tide of the massive ground invasion. Hitler himself put the defense commissioner Franconia Karl Holz in charge of the German forces protecting Nuermberg. Bamberg fell on April 15th. That meant we were next.

Oma sensed it was a time of desperation among the remaining ranks of the German army. Reports were circulating that soldiers were being massacred in growing numbers since the Allies were gaining ground. Every available man was sent to the front to fight. In letters to all the men in the family still fighting the war, Oma would write about the last, desperate acts a soon-to-be defeated army might employ. She warned them that the officers would force the wounded and non-combatants to fight to their deaths.

The 7th Army was poised to attack from the north and the east, defying conventional German defense thinking. As the Army neared Nuremberg, despite being heavily outnumbered, Holz devised a plan that involved setting up anti-tank barriers as well as anti-aircraft guns around the old city. He still held firmly to the belief that the Americans would break sooner or later when faced with his supposed superior forces. Nuremberg would not fall easily.

The final battle began on April 16, 1945. It would last for almost five days. This battle saw some of the fiercest combat during the war. A loss would mean a big blow to the morale of the remaining German army, since Nuremberg was a center of the Nazi regime. Because the German defenses proved so unrelenting, air-bombardment was again called for. The battle devastated the city.

It seemed as if it would never end, but we could hear the fighting all around us, sometimes distant, and other times a few blocks away.

Uncle Hans, my godfather, was a cook who never fired a gun during the war with the exception of his truncated training. During the duration of his service, he was always posted in the surrounding region, relatively close to home and far from the front lines, serving either the rear guard or the army hospitals. When the miltitary's strategic plan shifted, just as his mother had predicted,

Hans's unit was shifted, likely near the front at this time, perhaps forty miles from Nemenburg.

We later learned that during the last remaining days of fighting in April 1945, before Nuremberg capitulated, all hospital military personnel were given a rifle and told to fight to the end. In her letters, my grandmother instructed him to run should the fighting get so bad that they needed him to take up arms.

She also knew that any German soldier retreating in such a fashion would get shot by either side regardless of the circumstances, no matter how close to the end the war was. She begged him to ditch his uniform for civilian clothes if he could find them. If he was fortunate enough to make it home, we were prepared to give him the fresh suit hanging in the closet the second he came through the door. In her dreams and in her prayers, she implored him to do what he must to survive.

On that fateful evening of April 18, 1945, Oma went to bed early. The sun was just setting when all of the sudden she let out a blood curdling shriek which woke the entire house. All of us rushed to her room in our nightgowns. She was sitting up and appeared to be in a trance. We were transfixed, despite being used to her antics by now.

She was mumbling, incoherently at first.

Then she screamed with her eyes transfixed straight ahead. "Run, Hans. Run! Keep moving! Come to me, Hans. Come to me!"

This went on for what felt like hours but was probably only a few minutes. Suddenly, she stopped. Then she opened her eyes wide, her head fell back, she yelled some gibberish and dropped down onto the bed.

A few seconds of silence elapsed. Then she opened her eyes again, sat up and said in a tone so lifeless, I will never shake it, "Hans is dead."

At this point, we knew better than to disagree with her. She was right. Of course she was right! As we sat on her bed, she explained that she had seen him sprinting across a park. He was ducking between trees and bushes, and all the while bullets were flying over his head. He was zigzagging and trying to get to the other side. Finally, he made it. He raced down a city street and started to bang on door after door, begging to be let in. Every German citizen knew, due to the leaflets that had been dropping for weeks, that it was forbidden to give aid or shelter to soldiers. The penalty could be death. His begging was met by frightened citizens who refused to let him in.

He made it halfway down the block, pounding on each door with no success. Without notice, an armored jeep with a machine gunner affixed to the top saw him as they drove by his street. They quickly backed up, and in an instant, the turret housing a 50mm machine gun rotated and opened fire. He attempted to spin away as he was hit but died on the stoop.

Crestfallen as she was, Grandma got up, went into the kitchen, and eerily, without a sound, started to boil water for tea as if nothing had happened. For months, not another word was spoken about this incident. We knew there was nothing to discuss.

On the evening of the 20th of April, it was all over. The American flag was hoisted at Adolf Hitler Platz, formally ending the battle.

A few uneventful days of boredom passed when suddenly we heard distant cannon fire late in the afternoon. Although most of the fighting was over, a few lingering skirmishes still ensued. With every percussion, it appeared to get closer. The ground under our feet began to incessantly shake. By mid-evening, the horizon was ablaze with explosions and fire. Despite the surrender, yet again we no longer felt safe within our city limits.

One of my mother's sisters, who had lived with us previously, now lived about a half-hour walk away, south of the old city where fighting had been sparse. Somehow, she'd found an apartment house that was part of a factory owned by Americans. She came to visit us and suggested that the women and children come to live with her until the war was over. She told us the apartment manager had received a plaque inscribed *Off Limits, American Property*. How he got that is still a mystery to this day. My mother accepted the offer and the two of us followed my aunt to her home. We brought some clothes and what little food we had. It didn't take much effort to pack.

We moved in with my Aunt Frieda and her two children, my cousins. More days slowly passed by, bringing the distant noises of war ever closer. Aunt Frieda's house was in the middle of a block off of Main Street.

As we believed that there was still the possibility of some lingering skirmishes, it was decided we would put up the protective sign, barricade the front door, black out all the windows and hunker down in the basement.

One morning, we noticed that three German soldiers had barricaded themselves on the corner of our block. Clearly, they didn't know the city had fallen. Mama knew it was risky, but she decided to go out and pump them for any information and find out why they hadn't surrendered. Also, maybe they knew my father. A long shot, for sure. They simply didn't believe a surrender had occurred.

For several days, she went out to their make-shift-fort to make small talk and share a little food and water with them. They said they had received orders to fight until the very end, even if that meant death. To my young and innocent mind, it seemed foolish to keep fighting like this. They would simply be killed for no reason. What could three hungry and desperate soldiers do to stop the inevitable?

Nobody came to see them. There were no visits by ranking officers, as none were left. There were no reinforcements or replenishments of food or ammunition. They were completely isolated, and yet there they stayed, performing their duty. Up to the last day, the women tried to convince them to come into the house. They offered them civilian clothes, but the soldiers could not be reasoned with, considering it to be treason.

About a week later, I was suddenly awoken one night by some small arms fire and one very large explosion. We knew instinctively that the target was the small encampment down the street. Our worst fears were confirmed when the next day my mom took advantage of a lull in the fighting and found that all three soldiers had been killed and were still in their bunker, which was now riddled with bullets. We waited another three days for the coast to clear and then we all went out together--two moms and three kids with one neighbor. We had some old blankets and sheets and the women climbed over the sand bags and wrapped the bodies up. Collectively, we all helped carry them out. We walked across the street to the church courtyard, dug a shallow grave and buried them. It took us almost all afternoon. One of the men was 65 years old, and the other two could not have been older than 16 or 17. Truly the sign of a declining fighting force. Such a waste!

For two more days, we waited in the darkness and dampness while we heard ongoing skirmishes in a park about ten blocks away. Then followed an eerie silence from late in the afternoon to early in the morning. Perhaps once again the fighting had ended.

We were all anxious to find out what had transpired. My ever curious mother had an insatiable desire to look outside to see what was going on, despite the inherent dangers and the warning written on the leaflets. She found a rickety old stool and climbed up to the basement transom window, which was right under the ceiling and at the sidewalk level. She pushed back the shades and opened the window and stuck her head out. At that exact moment, a woman across the street also stuck her head out of her transom window, and they struck up a conversation. My mother could converse with the best of them.

She introduced herself and said, "My three children are starving, given that for the last week all we had to eat were a few raw potatoes and some flavorless soup."

The woman said, "My name is Agnes, and it is just me and my husband hiding in our basement. We have a limited stash of food, but I could certainly spare a couple of eggs for some starving children. But you would have to brave the danger and come and get them."

Agnes even offered to prepare them for us any way we wanted! This was especially enticing, considering we had no means to cook.

My mother with her ever-present humor yelled back, "We prefer our eggs fried! Just give me the heads up and I'll come over and get them."

Mother convinced all of us that this was worth the risk. But we needed a plan, and it had to be precise. The adults huddled and hatched a plan. First, my aunt was to move the barricade on the door. Agnes was told to signal when the eggs were ready. Mama stood a few feet back from the threshold, waiting. I was the lookout in the basement and peered carefully out of the transom window. When I saw Agnes wave a handkerchief, I yelled upstairs that the eggs were ready. My aunt opened the door and Mama took off running. She hurdled down the hallway, jumped from the stoop, ran as fast as she could across the street and then jumped through their door. Agnes closed the door immediately. Part One was successful.

Of course, everyone in our house was curious to watch the event unfold, so we stuck our heads out the windows both upstairs and down. Just as the door closed behind my mother as she entered Agnes's house, we felt an immediate surge of panic as we saw a huge tank with a star on it rumble down the cross street two blocks away. We recognized that it was an American tank and watched it slowly pull into the intersection. Part Two was now in jeopardy.

Not adhering to his role in Part Two, Agnes's husband didn't notice us waving frantically to abort. Instead, he opened the door and my mother's outstretched arm holding a frying pan appeared. We continued to wave our arms and scream at my mother, but it was too late! Adrenaline clearly had the best of her. She was undeterred. With her arm completely stretched out holding the frying pan at the end of it, she started to sprint as fast as she could back across our street. She had made it about a third of the way when the tank gunner recognized some movement. We all watched with bated breath as the turret slowly started to turn in her direction.

At this point, Mother sensed the danger and instinctively knew she was at the point of no return. She never took her eyes off the prize. If anything, she quickly picked up the pace. As if she were a woman possessed, she leapt through the open door and kept on running all the way down the hallway, her momentum causing her to crash into the far wall. Just as soon as she got through the door, we all yelled at my aunt and she closed the door with the swiftness of being pursued by the devil himself. Not a second elapsed before machine gun fire strafed the building's exterior, sending ricocheting shrapnel all over the streets.

We deliberately focused back on my mother. There she was, sitting on the floor, rhythmically panting as if to the beat of a drum, looking panicked. But the eggs were intact. It took a few seconds but we all collectively burst out into frantic, unstoppable laughter. What a relief!

When the laughter subsided, we replaced the barricades and closed the shades, which coincided with a loud bang on the door. Still shaking from the near-death experience, my aunt reluctantly opened the door and found herself staring inches away from the muzzles of several rifles. The rest of us had moved to the rear of the hallway and instinctively threw our arms up. An American soldier asked in broken German, "What is going on and why the sign outside?"

She explained that the building was owned by an American company and was under an order of protection. She then produced a document in English saying as much. The GI examined it closely as we all trembled.

He seemed to relax a bit and asked why someone ran across the street and disappeared through this door. My mother, who was still in the hallway holding the frying pan, stepped forward to show the evidence. The soldier smiled and did something unbelievable…he winked as we turned to see my mother, looking rather disheveled and holding the still steaming eggs in the frying pan. The soldier laughed, reached into a pouch at his waist, and produced several chocolate bars for us three children. He handed them over and said with a sarcastic smirk, "Foolish woman!"

He then turned and left.

After a few seconds, it occurred to us what had just happened and we once again burst into laughter. We'd pulled off the great egg caper and had received some American chocolate as the icing on the cake. It was a prelude that American GIs would be our saviors.

Once the threat abated and the fear subsided, excitement set in. This was our first encounter with Americans. He looked like a normal, everyday man, and he was humane, to boot. Delighted and animated, we were all talking at once as we returned to the basement and told the tale to the rest of the people who were taking shelter with us. My mother became an instant hero.

Never had fried eggs tasted so good! We all agreed that it had been worth the effort. My mother laughed and sarcastically said, "Sure, it wasn't you who almost got your butt shot off!" We laughed along with her, perhaps the first real glee any of us had felt in months.

CHAPTER FOURTEEN

The Omnipresence of GIs

Although the official surrender happened a few weeks before, it was still just a hopeful rumor as far as we were concerned, as accurate news traveled slower. A day or two after the *Great Egg Caper,* jeeps with loudspeakers attached to their roofs rolled through the streets and, in perfect German, civilians were told they needed to stay indoors until further notice. The next day, the jeeps returned, this time informing all citizens that the city of Nuremberg had surrendered. Tempered excitement began to bubble up in our apartment and then spread to the streets as we all came out for a short period of time to hug our neighbors, our expressions mixed with tears and smiles. Although the fighting may have ended, the hardships would persist as we had little food and water. The next day, our burden was lifted slightly when the electricity returned, making our life so much easier.

Three days after that, it was announced that there would be a curfew to control the last remaining fighting. The citizens of Nuremberg would be allowed outside between the hours of 6:00 a.m. and 6:00 p.m. As kids, we couldn't wait to get back outside. We were all going stir-crazy. A few days after the ceasefire, my mother and I moved back into my grandmother's place in the center of town.

The American GI presence made an immediate impact on our city. Within a day of the surrender, a few hundred troops rolled into town. The American army took over the schoolhouse down the street and turned it into both a barracks and headquarters. I saw an opportunity to help the family out, so I started to hang out in front of the schoolhouse waiting for the GIs. Bashfully, a few friends and I tried to make contact with some of the soldiers. We found them to be very friendly and engaging. They seemed at ease and content. They appeared to enjoy our company and gave us chocolate and chewing gum whenever we showed up. What a treat! I had never tasted gum before and promptly swallowed the first stick after a few chews. The soldiers got a big kick out of this and enjoyed a few belly laughs. Two others reached into their pockets and gave us a few more sticks of gum. This time, through non-verbal communication, they gave us instructions on how to actually chew the gum. Even the simple process of chewing gum was foreign to us!

Not long after, I befriended a couple of young soldiers and we figured out a way to communicate. I got permission from my mother and grandparents to invite them to our place for coffee. Why not try to get details on the latest developments since the fighting had stopped?

The next day, two soldiers knocked on our door. One was tall with dark hair and the other short and a bit pudgy. We all sat around the kitchen table. My mom served some weak coffee and stale bread. It was difficult to communicate with them, but with them knowing some German and me knowing a few English words by now, we were actually able to converse. We had a nice visit, which lasted about fifteen minutes.

After some kind words mixed with body language to fill in the gaps, the GIs got up and said goodbye. I believe it struck them how poor we were and how little we had, especially with five kids staring at them from the fringes with gaunt and dirty faces. On their next visit a few days later, they brought coffee and some of their C-rations. They also asked if my mother could do laundry for them. She agreed, but only if they would provide soap. She made it clear that she would certainly welcome the work AND the money.

The next morning, I waited at the schoolhouse gate and sure enough, one of the GIs showed up with a rather large laundry bag. He indicated he wanted it back in two days at the same time and the same place. I brought the bag home, and we emptied it on the kitchen table. It contained underwear, socks, handkerchiefs, and a huge bar of brown soap. What really got our attention was the sight of a few chocolate bars and a carton of cigarettes. We thought we were in heaven. While the chocolate bars were a real treat for all of us kids, the carton of cigarettes was the real jackpot, since you could trade them for almost anything on the black market--butter, eggs, meat, and more.

As I got into the laundry-delivery business, I saw an opportunity to embrace capitalism and swiftly became an entrepreneur. Since no one in my family had a job, there was no income coming in. We had a short meeting as a family to figure out how we could sustain ourselves. Duties were delegated. It was decided that my mother, her two sisters, and my 17-year-old cousin Lilo (short for Lisa Lotte) would continue to do the laundry. My cousin Robert was assigned to go to the main railroad yard every morning to see what came in on the cattle cars that delivered rations and supplies to the GIs. Sometimes the procurement officer would "drop" some cans of Spam and other items. If that didn't produce results, when no one was looking he would scamper up and "pick-off" whatever he could carry. My other cousin Paul was old enough to get a job with the American army guarding facilities such as barracks, motor tools, and munitions.

My assignment was to pick up the laundry, generally interface with the GIs, and hang around the barracks, waiting for anything they might want to give away. It was up to me to bring home anything edible or of value that we could swap on the black market. When the GIs took over my schoolhouse, the first thing they did was build an incinerator in the back yard. There was a large structure made of brick, about 30 by 30 feet, and maybe 5 feet high. A few of the other neighborhood boys and I would climb the wall from the other side every day at mealtime, waiting for the soldiers on kitchen duty to dump their 50-gallon drums of garbage and leftovers. After their drums had been emptied, we would jump into the structure and rescue anything that was edible or useful. I would always return home with a bag of partially eaten toast, remnants of canned Spam, pieces of steak or bacon, and leftover rations.

Between meals, I would scout out the grounds of the schoolhouse, collecting cigarette butts or chewing gum. The stockyard fence kept us at bay, but I begged my grandfather for a metal stick I knew he could get through some of his friends. I felt as if I were the luckiest kid when he was able to secure the longest stick in the neighborhood. I was always the most successful, stretching through the fence with my long spear to skewer partially smoked cigarettes and discarded gum. When I returned home, I would unravel all the cigarette butts and reclaim all the remaining tobacco. I would turn over the gum to my mother and she would boil it and then soak it in sugar. Both products were quite valuable in the burgeoning black market trade.

As an enterprising young man, I would occasionally do favors or run errands for the GIs. One day, a very profitable opportunity presented itself. About a mile from our house was a rather large lake in our public park which had several small islands. Before the war, it was an idyllic tourist attraction. The boat-rental business had just reopened. It quickly became a popular place for the soldiers to visit when they had a bit of R&R time.

The GIs liked to take their German sweethearts out onto the lake to one of the islands. It was quite picturesque and romantic. As I made a habit of hanging around the lake towards the end of the day, the soldiers began to pay me to escort the romantically inclined twosome. I'd row while the couple would sit on the other side of the boat and make out. Since I had to sit facing them, I got quite an education as a young gondolier.

The world's oldest profession also got a rebirth under my purview. Due to my relationship with a number of friendly GIs, I became their chief intermediary. From time to time, I would assist a lady of the evening in negotiating with a GI for a "ride" on the boat. It came to be that I was able to make money from all aspects of this arrangement. First, I would help negotiate the terms of the transaction. Then the GI would pay me a few German marks to row the boat out to the islands. When their evening ended, the GI would then leave the boat on the other side of the lake, since it was closer to their barracks. The boat rental operator would then pay me to retrieve the abandoned boats and row them back to the pavilion. And last but not least, the working girls would give me a tip for helping seal the deal. On a good day, I was the most profitable member of the family. Little did I realize that I was now a participant in the pimping business at the tender age of ten. I certainly didn't let my mother in on the deal-making skills I had developed!

CHAPTER FIFTEEN

Boys Being Boys

One nice summer day after the war ended, a few friends and I decided to take a hike to the ruins of the ammunition factory at the edge of the city. When we arrived there, we found the factory surrounded by a fence and completely boarded up. The building had been heavily bombed during the fighting and fires had raged on for several days before self-extinguishing and leaving a blackened shell of a warehouse in its place. There were signs hanging on the fence warning of the dangers and imploring civilians to stay out. We were undeterred. Of course that didn't apply to us!

In fact, we were hell-bent on finding some ammo and soon found a way to get in undetected. We rummaged around inside the few remaining walls but found no ammunition. The floor and walls were splattered with the telltale signs of exploded ammunition crates. We kept searching and came across a room that had some unopened crates still neatly stacked. We were able to crack one crate open, and to our amazement and joy, we found beautiful black boxes, 5 by 12 and 1 thick with snaps to hold the lids closed. Inside, in neatly arranged indentations, we found dozens of firing caps. Their purpose was to be thrust into the bottom of a large munition shell and loaded into a cannon, where the hammer would strike and propel the deadly projectile. We opened more crates and found different-sized caps, all neatly arranged, as well. We were elated and stuffed our shirts and pockets with as many caps as we could.

We didn't yet know what we were going to do with them, but we figured we'd find a way to have some fun. When we got back to our neighborhood, one of our friends suggested that we lay them on the granite cobblestone and hit them with a hammer. We quickly learned just how dangerous that was as we felt the stinging of tiny brass fragments hit our face, chest, and arms.

Another suggested putting them on the curbstone and letting a brick fall on them. Soon, we were bleeding from all the cuts and scrapes on our ankles and shins from this activity. Obviously, we weren't very intelligent when it came to munitions. We had to find a better way. That's when I came up with an idea--to lay them on a streetcar track and see what happened. The streetcar connecting Nuremberg with Furth, a neighboring town, had just had its service restored.

The two-car train passed by the schoolhouse about every 20 minutes. We placed a few caps on the rail line about one yard apart. We crossed the street and sat on a stoop as we waited for the train to come. Much to our amazement, the caps exploded like small firecrackers. It sounded like several 20 caliber rifles going off in rapid fire.

Soon we learned that by placing the caps on the rail and varying the distance between the caps, we could achieve a rhythmic pattern of pops. Being musically inclined, we adapted the placement and size of the caps which resulted in an explosive symphony. As we experimented with our placement well into the evening, spectators filled the windows of the schoolhouse. The American soldiers obviously enjoyed the orchestral coordination of the pops on the strip of track several hundred feet in length.

Out of nowhere, an American soldier approached me, clearly enjoying the show. He pointed to the tracks and handed me several small pouches. These pouches were about one to one-and-a-half inches wide and one-half inch thick. A thin copper band could be folded out from the two ends. It seemed to me that these munition pouches would enhance the entertainment. I placed a few of them about every tenth cap.

There was one pouch much bigger than the rest. It measured two by four inches and was much thicker. I decided that it would probably sound best if positioned last and provide the climax. I strategically placed it at the end of the long string of caps, and we waited anxiously for the next streetcar to arrive. It was worth the wait. The pattern of pops was breathtaking. With the combination of caps and pouches, it sounded like, pop-pop-pop-boom, pop-pop-pop-boom, and when the front wheel of the track got to the end of the string, it was pop-pop-pop-bang.

It provided the climax we were expecting, triggering quite a large explosion with sparks flying everywhere. The train came to a sudden stop. Smoke was billowing out from under the lead car. Passengers were jumping off the train, screaming in panic.

Oh no! What had we done? We ran as fast as we could along the schoolhouse fence, disappearing around the corner. The last thing I heard as we escaped was all of the American GIs cheering, clapping, and hysterically laughing. We were afraid to be seen anywhere near the tracks for several days after that. We disposed of the remaining caps by throwing them into a fire which we'd built inside the ruins of a bombed-out house. But that's another story altogether.

The months following the fall of Nuremberg and then the subsequent end of the war were probably the most exciting for me and my friends. We could get into all kinds of trouble, mainly the mischievous kind, without fear of getting caught. Trouble just seemed to find us! Security in the city mainly consisted of the American military police, sometimes accompanied by a newly-hired German police officer. Other than that, the city was a free-for-all! Our playground was the ruins of the bombed-out city. It was quite a challenge to roam around the walled castle, climbing the upper stories despite the lack of stairs. More often than not, our escapades were very risky, since most of what remained of the walls and floors were unstable at best and crumbling at worst. Since we had no toys to play with, however, anything we found became a source of amazement and amusement.

When all of us scamps weren't working to help our families, one of our favorite activities was searching for and collecting shrapnel, which came in all shapes, colors and sizes. Trading it with friends was great fun. The more bizarre and colorful the piece, the greater its value. I used to carry a shoe box full of shrapnel and actively traded it on a daily basis. We searched incessantly for all types of weapons and ammunition. Among my group of friends, we had quite a collection of rifles, pistols, and even a machine gun. Fortunately, most of these weapons were jammed or broken, although we tried hard to refurbish them, with little success.

One day while searching the ruins of a house, we found a loaded flare gun. And of course, without much thought, we decided to fire it. The building we were in lacked a roof, so I fired it straight up in the air. Suddenly we heard screaming. We looked out one of the windows and realized that the flare had landed on the wooden roof of an old house down the street and set it on fire. We hot-tailed it out of the building before anybody could recognize that we were responsible for the mishap. We ran to my house and hid in the basement, giggling and reveling in our exploits. Fortunately, the fire was swiftly extinguished and no real harm was done. We were turning into quite a band of rascals and hooligans.

During another beautiful summer day, some friends and I had gone to the inner city on a search-and-find mission. As we sifted through the rubble of yet another bombed out building, I came across an American grenade rifle, or as we knew it, a *Panzerfaust*, or a tank fist. It's purpose was to disable a tank, so it was quite powerful. What a discovery! And to boot, it had what looked like a grenade or a warhead still stuck in the front of the tube! Well, this was definitely the discovery of all discoveries for a rogue group of bored and inquisitive scoundrels.

The question quickly became where we could fire this weapon and what could we fire it at? We certainly knew we couldn't transport it too far, as some adult would surely see us and take it away. It was over 3 feet long and had a 200-foot firing range. Since the city was encircled by a huge wall with a moat protecting it, we decided that this would be a great target. We carefully climbed down thirty feet into the moat. Four of us were holding this tube under our arms, afraid it might go off if we jostled it too much. We got to the bottom and aimed the weapon toward the city wall. We weren't convinced that we could withstand the recoil a rifle this size might create, so we needed a plan. The four of us formed a straight line facing the direction of the target with the tube on our shoulders. We backed up against the outer wall of the moat to absorb the expected kick. I was in front of this line up and the kid behind me was supposed to pull the trigger on the count of three. The other two boys at the rear were to help support the tube as well as brace us against the wall. We collectively counted, "One, two, three," and the grenade went off with an enormous explosion. We all fell to the ground, dazed and confused.

The two guys who were holding the tube in the back were screaming. It felt as if my ears had exploded. The heat the weapon created was overwhelming, and there was dust and debris everywhere. We immediately realized we had done something very wrong! People above the moat were yelling down at us.

As we scrambled back to our feet, we saw what had happened. First, there was a big hole in the wall about 20 feet in front of us from the explosion. It was about 3 feet in diameter and about 2 feet deep. The two guys who were holding the back of the tube were now holding their heads and crying. Little did we know that this weapon had no recoil, but in-fact contained a huge fiery backflash. When this flash hit the wall behind us, it bounced back, burning the hair off of their heads as well as singeing all of our necks. The last guy got it the worst. His head was steaming, and his ears and neck were reddish-blue. He had very little hair left. Since I was in front, I'd been wounded the least, with just a little singeing of my neck, ears, and hair.

Since the witnesses above continued to scream down at us and point in our direction, we intuitively knew we would face some civic backlash. We ignored the pain and ran along the moat as fast as we could. Fortunately, this was our playground and we knew our way around. We found a way to climb out and quickly disappeared.

For the next few weeks, we all walked around with a heavy coat of salve on our ears and necks and we all wore hats to hide our burns and disguise our identities.

As our wounds healed and our hair grew back, we came to fully realize how foolish we'd been and swore to each other that we would be wiser and more careful the next time.

During this time of reorganization and rebuilding, our band of rascals was free to roam the city as we saw fit, since adults had bigger issues with which to contend. It didn't take long before trouble found us once again. Resuming our search and recovery mission, we would stumble upon unspent ammunition on a daily basis.

On one such occasion, we found about ten 30mm caliber rounds still in the case. One of my friends foolishly suggested that we should see what these explosives could do. As naïve as we continued to prove to be, we went to his house when no one was home. Ignoring our protests, he threw them into his mother's cooking oven. It took a little while before the rounds exploded, but when they did, we all ducked for cover. Based on our grenade experience, we half expected the oven to blow up. Fortunately, it was a cast iron stove, so the bullets kept ricocheting around inside the oven, causing quite the ruckus, but no one got hurt. That is, until his mom came running in to find out what had exploded. She gave us all quite a swift swat on the backside with her wooden cooking spoon.

The welt made it too painful to sit for a few days, but given the alternative, we took our punishment. Based on that experience, we decided to be a bit more creative with our stash.

Someone suggested we pry the bullets off the shells and collect the gunpowder. By the time we were done, we had a paper bag filled with two pounds of gunpowder from our huge stockpile. Then the question came up: "How do we get rid of gunpowder?"

I suggested we burn it. So off we went, half-cocked once again, armed with a bag of gunpowder and matches. We went into a bombed-out ruin and formed a nice cone-shaped pile of gunpowder. I told everybody to take a step back. I lit a match and laid it on the pile, thinking it would burn.

Once again, we grossly miscalculated! Instead of burning, it exploded, sending a flash of fire straight up into the air. Feeling the heat burning my face, I jumped back. Although the blast and subsequent flash only lasted a second, when the smoke cleared, my friends could see that I had no eyelashes, no eyebrows and no hair in the front of my head. They buckled over, laughing hysterically. It only took me a second, and then I burst out laughing, too. My face was hot to the touch and my friends told me I looked as if I had a bad sunburn. I had to endure the scrutiny and scolding of my family, since they were always trying to corral us. Perhaps when I wasn't looking they were giggling at my plight, since it was a bit lighthearted in the house after each stupid thing I did. They just couldn't control us, and after a while they stopped trying. I had to shoulder another few weeks of salve and wearing hats. So much for learning from our past mistakes!

CHAPTER SIXTEEN

Firsts

I owe many of my lifetime firsts to the influx of so many GIs. I believe the American soldiers were just as happy as we were that the war was over, and they enjoyed the simple pleasure of sharing this exuberance with all of us youngsters. This new world offered us so many ways to see things differently. One day, as I hung around the schoolhouse gate as usual, I watched the GIs to see what they were up to. I spotted one soldier about to open a Coca-Colabottle. He glanced at me and must have seen my astonished look as I stood there bug-eyed. I had never seen a Coca-Cola before. He must have felt bad, because he slowly lowered the bottle toward me and gestured for me take it.

My friends and I sought out any new experience we could find, and there were no boundaries. I had to be shrewd if I was to enjoy this experience alone. I took the bottle, hid it under my jacket, and ran as fast as I could toward my house. Sensing my excitement, I was followed by two of my more envious friends. In the days of scarcity, whenever luck was bestowed upon you by a GI, you had to hide it and get away quickly. Otherwise, older kids and bullies would take your find away from you. It boiled down to survival of the fittest.

When I got to my house, I ran into the basement, huffing and puffing and out of breath from my mad dash. I was so excited I barely noticed anyone behind me. They were right on my heels. As our house was one with an open door policy, no one thought it strange that I was being hotly pursued. Once I got there, I assessed my dilemma. I had no bottle opener. I figured I had a small window of opportunity before my friends pounced on me. I looked around and acted impulsively, as kids often do. I just hit the corner of the wall with the bottle as if I was christening a majestic ship. The neck flew off just above the impact point, leaving sharp, jagged edges. Because of all the running and jostling, the carbonation caused the soda to spew out of the opening. Knowing I had little or no time to enjoy this, I hastily put the broken top of the bottle into my mouth, tasting the sugary elixir.

One of my friends came sprinting down the stairs and was obviously anxious to participate in this unlikely endeavor. Unwittingly, he grabbed the bottle while it was still in my mouth and yanked it as hard as he could screaming, "What have you got there?"

As to be expected, the violent nature of the yank caused the jagged edge of the bottle to cut my entire upper lip. Blood mixed with the Coke and subsequent pain should have followed. But it didn't, as the pleasure of such an exotic and tasty elixir mitigated the suffering after all. I did pay the price, however, as it took a week for my lip to heal, which made eating nearly impossible.

CHAPTER SEVENTEEN

Rebuilding

A few months after the war ended, work crews began to clear the rubble from the streets. These crews were conscripted from the surrounding area and were guaranteed payment. This was a prelude to the European Recovery Plan (Marshall Plan) which wasn't officially eneacted until 1948. It was an effort to rebuild the war-torn country, put people back to work, and thwart the spreading of communism.

However, the relief effort needed to get started quickly, as thousands had been left homeless or fragile. If you were able-bodied and could work, you could put food on your table by participating in the city's rebuilding process. Within the walls of the inner city, crews began laying small-scale railroad tracks. Lorries, similar to the ones used in mines, were installed on the tracks to carry the dirt, debris, and bricks out of the city. Every brick was numbered and tagged to identify the exact location where it was found. The concept was to re-use the very same bricks to restore each and every building to its pre-war grandeur.

There was serious consideration given to completely bulldozing all the buildings that were deemed damaged beyond repair, but wise voices overrode those who were looking for an expeditious and probably cheaper solution. All around West Germany, plans were devised to rebuild these once-great cities. In Communist or East Germany, no such plans were discussed, never mind expedited. Buildings lay in ruins there for years, if not decades. Cultural icons and architectural ideals were of no importance to the Russians.

One morning we awoke to noises out on our street. We lived out by the city walls, and no tracks had yet been laid. We looked out the window and saw that on the far side of the rubble which had clogged our street, army trucks had pulled up and about thirty men in tattered German army uniforms had been unloaded. They were armed with picks and shovels and began the laborious task of loading the dump trucks with the numbered rocks and bricks. Each one of these men had white POW marks on their backs.

This was a revelation! Almost immediately, my family and many of our neighbors clamored over to meet the German soldiers. They were like celebrities. All at once, everyone screamed at the soldiers. It was bedlam.

"Where were you stationed? What was it like? Is it truly over? Is anyone hungry? Thirsty? Have you ever heard from or seen in your passing _____?" (Fill in the blank with any number of missing men from our town).

However, the few American soldiers guarding them were a bit leery of our intrusion and kept us away as best they could. We knew we needed a plan! Over the next day or two, my friends and I managed to weasel our way in and befriend the American guards. Eventually, they relented and allowed us to visit with the German POW soldiers while they were on break. The Americans couldn't resist our youthful charms.

I inquired if the POWs would like something to eat or drink, such as bread and water.

One prisoner spoke up and confirmed, "We are treated very well by our American captors and receive ample nourishment from US rations. What we really want is some authentic German food such as potato soup."

I ran home and told my mother. She immediately jumped to action organizing the neighbors. Soon, word got around, and despite our less-than-full cupboards, the women had several large pots of potato soup prepared and ready to go.

As the organized procession of German housewives carrying the pots of soup made its way down the street and across the rubble, a couple of guards stopped them to ask what this was all about. A prisoner who spoke some English told them that these women had made soup for them. The guards motioned for the women to bring the pots to the back of the trucks. A guard whistled, and all the German prisoners gathered around the pots. They filled their army-issued tin cups with warm potato soup, and pretty soon a festive spirit overcame the gathering. The women ambled among the prisoners, dishing out soup and amiably laughing with them.

All of a sudden, a friendly guard walked over to my mother, who was holding a large pot. He asked to taste it, dipped his cup into the pot, and sipped a small sample of soup. By the telltale look on his face, I knew he was not too impressed. We all knew the soup lacked salt and had no taste since spices were rare. He said nothing, but smiled.

The next morning, as usual, the truck arrived carrying the POWs. Once again, all the kids gathered around the guards, looking for candy and gum handouts. One guard that I recognized beckoned me to the side of a truck and handed me a cardboard box. He said, "Soup!" and gestured for me to take the box home. I understood and ran home before anyone could see what was happening. In the box, my mom found an ample supply of salt, Spam, pork rinds, and crackers, all ingredients we had not seen in some time.

My mother spread the word through the verbal news channel and almost instantly the women of the neighborhood gathered once again in our kitchen to prepare the pots of potato soup. This time, the soup was flavored with salt and the rest of the ingredients from the box. What an improvement! I was the official soup taster. The soup was savory and quite delicious! I couldn't remember the last time I'd had soup, or any food, for that matter, that had this much flavor.

As the procession of women carried the pots out to the truck at noon time, the guards immediately came over to inspect the end product. The guard who'd given me the box was the first to dip his cup into the pot, and as he did so, he winked at me. He tasted the soup and his face lit up. "All right," he exclaimed, and blew his whistle. The rest of the guards and the prisoners came and filled their cups. Soon, a loud cheer echoed through the street. Even the guards chimed in. Everybody loved the soup. The festive atmosphere continued for a good hour before the men had to go back to work.

For the next few days, the American guards brought all kinds of provisions, including bread, bacon and spices, indulgences we hadn't seen in years. This allowed the women to do what they did best and make good use of all this newfound culinary luxury. The well-fed men worked even harder with their stomachs full, and the American guards saw the benefits to their charity. It was a win for all concerned, and it eased a lot of tension in our town.

Unfortunately, after a few weeks, the guards told us this was the last day that the prisoners would be in the neighborhood. After many cheers, thanks, tears, and hugs, we waved goodbye to the departing soldiers and yes, even the guards! They'd left an indelibly positive mark on all our young and impressionable minds.

Between the local labor and the POWs, a great deal of the rubble from the city was removed in a short period of time, making it a lot more efficient to move around the neighborhood.

By the end of 1945, the American army vacated the schoolhouse. All the neighborhood children were asked to help restore the classrooms for normal school use. I remember seeing all the tables and chairs piled up in the hallway. As we lifted and moved the desks back into the classrooms, our fingers felt something foreign underneath each one. Once in the classroom, we discovered the underside of the blackboard covered with the same substance. The GIs had stuck their chewing gum to the underside of all the furniture. Although conditions were improving, luxuries like gum and candy were hard to come by. We pried off the gum from the furniture and went back into the business of boiling it and soaking it in warm sugar water. After a few days, it was chewable and tasty once again.

CHAPTER EIGHTEEN

The Castle

When we weren't tasked with finding or stealing provisions, my friends and I continued to explore the bombed-out churches and the old medieval walls and ruins, as well as the castle which sat on top of the highest point in the city. When the moat was filled with rainwater, we would float on 55-gallon drums, pretending to be marauding soldiers during the Crusades.

The castle was the ultimate playground and allowed us to use our imaginations. Early one morning, we found our way into the castle ruins and discovered stairways leading to an underground prison. We were enamored, to say the least. For days, we roamed the tunnels and hallways and discovered secret passages that connected the castle to many buildings, such as the old city hall, churches, and the fortifications surrounding the city. It soon became clear that the walls of this castle connected all the important buildings. In theory, if the city had been under attack during medieval times, the citizens could escape the skirmishes and hide beneath the city. I recall spending hours crawling and groping in the darkness with our hands, running them along cold and damp stone walls to feel our way around in the clammy darkness.

We could feel and sense the cold and eerie breezes coming up from the dark depths of the hallways. In those days, we didn't have flashlights and only carried a few matches, which were still considered luxuries. Therefore, we tried to save them for emergencies. Every so often, we would come to what seemed like an intersection of corridors. On one occasion, we spotted a glimmer of light, so we headed that direction. It turned out to be a horizontal air shaft, and looking out, we could determine what part of the city we were in. I was leading the group of three down a corridor with my hands, feeling my way along the walls, when it abruptly ended. A strange cool breeze gave us a chill, and we couldn't tell if we were at an intersection. I kicked some loose stones forward with my feet, and after what seemed like a half dozen seconds, I heard the sound of rocks splashing into water. It was time to light a match!

And thank God we did. A few feet ahead was the edge of a large circular hole with several corridors leading to it. It seemed we were at the well from which the prisoners would get their water. A heavy rope coming from above and disappearing into the depths below confirmed my suspicions. Any one of us could have fallen over a hundred feet had we not been so careful, or so we thought.

A few years later when the castle reopened for visitors, guided tours resumed. This section of the castle was called the *Tessa Brunens*, or Deep Fountain. Visitors would stand around the rim of the hole, about six feet in diameter, and a tray with lit candles would be lowered. From the light, one could see the corridor at various levels which led to the prison cells. This was the very same section I had explored a couple years earlier.

The real surprise occurred when the schools were reopened. We discovered, to our chagrin, just how deep it really was. Classes resumed a few months after the rebuilding effort began. School buildings were no longer needed to house American GIs or act as staging headquarters. As a way to renew our city pride, classes from our area and adjoining towns were invited to the castle on an official tour.

It was quite interesting to learn about the history and significance of the castle as it had protected the region during the Crusades. Our docent, who was quite conversant in the structure and architecture, asked a question of all of us.

"How deep do you think this well is?"

Students started their guessing at around 50 feet and ended at 200 feet. My intrepid friends and I kept our collective mouths shut while at the same time attempting to stifle our giggles. Since this was an educational trip, we could learn a new formula for calculating the depths. I was given the task of dropping a stone into the well and counting the seconds it took for the stone to hit the water. The docent then shouted out the calculation to determine the depth of the well. Everyone was shocked to learn that it was 900 feet deep. Our group of secret explorers went weak in the knees as we all smirked at each other. Thank God we had matches on us that day.

It was not only a miracle we survived the war. It was equally impressive that we outlived our youthful curiosity in the post-war reconstruction! If it wasn't the abandoned munitions that summoned us into danger, it was the dark corridors of the castle beckoning us to take just one more step.

CHAPTER NINETEEN

Reclaiming Lost Loved Ones

As spring turned to summer, civilians were allowed to be out on the streets again unimpeded by following months of curfew restrictions. Travel of all kinds was now allowed. All around, women were busy burying dead civilians and German soldiers when they were unearthed in the ruins. My grandmother became increasingly restless. She kept repeating that Hans, her oldest son, had been trying to get home at the end of the war when he'd been shot and killed. She knew he was still calling to her and she now wanted to bring him home. Oma became more and more determined to find her son. One day, she gathered her daughters and grandchildren, all five of us, and told us that early the next morning we were going to find Hans.

"He deserves a Catholic burial!" Oma decried.

We woke up early the next morning and began walking towards the hospital that we knew he'd last worked at, which was miles away. As the sun began to heat, up and down the streets we went, block after block. My grandmother led in the front and all of us followed like a flock of geese. She was driven by determination and became more and more tense the closer we came to the hospital. By late afternoon, we were walking along a park. THE PARK...she sensed it was from the night he'd died. My grandmother became extremely agitated. Her pace quickened. The park ended at a crossroad with houses on the other side facing the park.

Oma rang the doorbell of the first house on the corner. An old woman answered the door.

Grandma quickly inquired, "Was any fighting going on near the park during the last days of the war?"

The woman said "Yes, there was fighting in and around the park. We huddled in the rear of the house, praying for it all to end."

Grandma continued her line of questioning, "Had any German soldiers knocked or asked for help?"

The woman remembered that a couple of German soldiers had indeed knocked on the door asking to come in. You could tell she was devastated when she admitted they'd had to refuse to let them in out of fear of the American warning and the threat of death if they harbored any German soldiers.

My grandmother then went from door to door and was told the same story. Suddenly she got to the middle of the block and whispered almost to herself as she touched a door, "This is where Hans died."

This time a young boy opened the door and then called out for his grandfather. An elderly gentleman came to the door with his grandson peeking from benind his thigh. He told Oma that two soldiers were banging on the door and were screaming and begging to be let in while they cowered in the kitchen. He could hear two distinct voices.

"I was so tempted to go to them, but there was two of them and there were too many of us hiding inside, including my grandchildren. We were all shaking and crying in the kitchen. We just couldn't risk it. We are so sorry!"

He went on to say the next morning after the fighting had subsided, they found the two men dead on the stoop. Some of his neighbors from that block all got together and buried these men in the park down the street. My grandmother was visibly shaking and asked to be taken to the graves. She was led the half a block to the opening of the park.

As she stood at the gates staring across at the freshly distrurbed ground, she almost fainted.

"Hans is over there," she insisted as she pointed to the clearly defined mounds. She told us all to go search for shovels or anything that could help dig him up.

"I need to give him a righteous, Christian burial."

We did as we were told and went around the neighborhood borrowing shovels and a wagon while she sat on the grass muttering to herself.

We returned within an hour and began to dig. This was quite a physical undertaking for three women and five children to dig up two bodies. But after all we had been through and all that we had seen, it didn't feel abnormal. It was something we needed to do to make things right for Oma. She deserved closure.

When we reached the first body, we recognized right away that it was my uncle. In his chest pocket, we found the papers to confirm his ID, along with a picture of his girlfriend Clara. It was a sad, long, and arduous trip home, taking turns pulling him in the wagon. We didn't get home until way after midnight. We were exhausted.

The next day, Oma convinced the priest to come with us to the cemetery to give Hans the proper burial he deserved.

HAPTER TWENTY

Psychic Gifts

Although the war ended in the spring of 1945, for many months and even years afterward, many women continued to come to my grandmother's door to inquire about their husbands or sons, begging for any information or hope.

"Is he still alive?" was the common answer sought by all of them.

If our local soldiers had been captured by American, or Allied, forces, it wasn't soon after the war ended that these men marched home into their neighborhoods without warning and were welcomed by throngs of family and friends. They were all smiles and looked reasonably healthy given their circumstances.

However, if they'd been taken prisoner by the Russian army, they weren't so quick to return. For months that soon stretched to years, every so often out of nowhere a neighborhood man would just show up, a former POW most likely held by the Russians, clothed in nothing but rags, walking into town like a skeleton with death in his eyes. Rumors of who was still in these Russian camps raged on.

My two aunts were Frieda and Wilma. Aunt Frieda's husband, Onkel Fritz, was just such a prisoner of war. He'd been captured by the Russians on the eastern front and spent three years in Siberia working in a labor camp. One day he just walked into town. Oma always reassured her daughter Wilma that he was still alive, so she never gave up hope. Once again, Oma had a sense of his presence. He just emerged one day weighing 120 pounds, unshaven and sick looking. He walked with a limp, but he was welcomed back with no questions asked. In fact, for the rest of his life, he never uttered a word about his three years in captivity. In less than two months he was nursed back to health by a combination of love, ample helpings of good home cooking, and regular exercise of walking through town.

Women, both wives and mothers, would show up on my grandmother's doorstep every few days inquiring whether their husbands or sons, whom they were assuming were POWs, were still alive. Oma would read the Tarot cards or tea leaves. She would be honest even if the news wasn't good.

However, when appropriate, she would tell them, "Yes, your husband (or son) is alive and well. He is in a POW camp and will come home soon." She gave them hope.

This went on for several years after the war, but after a while fewer women came to see my grandmother as their loved ones either returned or were confirmed dead. This was actually quite a lucrative endeavor for our family. Most women had little or no money, but they were willing to barter what little they had for even a shred of information. We were the beneficiaries of fresh bread, eggs, cheese, salt, and the occasional live chicken for the hope my oma gave them.

One woman was very persistent. She showed up on Oma's doorstep at least three or four times a month, incessantly inquiring whether or not her husband was alive. This went on for years.

On every occasion, Oma always told her he was alive and well. She had clear visions of him each and every day she inquired.

One day in the summer of 1948, a full three years after the war ended, we were sitting in the kitchen having dinner when the doorbell rang. Oma suddenly stiffened and, like a zombie in a trance, walked to the door. It was a bit strange, and as was my custom, I followed her. She opened the door, and there stood that same woman, ready to ask the usual question.

Before the woman could even open her mouth, Grandma raised her hand, stopping her mid-sentence.

She said in a very solemn voice, "Go home. He is waiting for you."

The woman tried to say something, but my grandmother just kept her hand up and repeated, "Go home. He is waiting for you!"

Clearly confused and perhaps a bit excited, the woman stood there dumbfounded. After what seemed like an eternity, she turned and swiftly walked from our house with tears streaming down her cheeks. It was an experience I will never forget. Oma, instantly looking tired, closed the door and slowly shuffled back to the dinner table with me in tow. When she sat down, she closed her eyes and whispered, "Thank you, God. He is home!" We all sat there in silence.

Not even a half-hour later, the doorbell rang again. This time no one at the table moved. It was as if everyone had frozen in time, not able to once again understand Oma's clairvoyance. Finally, I got up and answered the door. Standing there in front of me was the woman with her husband. Even though he was nothing but skin and bones, sporting a full beard speckled with gray, his face emoted pure elation. Just as Oma had predicted, he was sitting on the doorstep waiting for his wife when she returned home. What a reunion that must have been! They both gave Oma a tight hug. The wife held the embrace forever, not wanting to let go. Oma's gift was a blessing to the entire town, but especially for this woman.

CHAPTER TWENTY-ONE

A New Life Begins

Even though the war had ended and food was more prevalent, Mama maintained her habit of going to bed early in the evening, continuing her mantra, "Go to bed early. When you sleep, you don't have hunger." It became clear that she had been sacrificing her rations for me and my cousins while we still all lived under one roof.

One night in July of 1945, we went to bed just as the sun set. We shared the same room and mom was telling a story about my father and how they first met. Suddenly, we heard footsteps outside the bedroom window. The familiar sound of military-issued boots with nail-studded soles gave us a chill and transported us back to the time of war. The footsteps stopped, and for some unexplained reason, we knew instinctively it was my dad. We sprang out of the bed and sprinted to the door before the doorbell rang. Indeed, my father was standing there. He stood before us still wearing a uniform, minus any military decoration. He looked skinny, pale, and drained. We could immediately tell he hadn't eaten in a while. But he was smiling from ear to ear.

Hugs and crying filled the air. It woke up the entire house. Everyone came out in their nightgowns and screamed and shrieked. The atmosphere was celebratory, to say the least. More hugs and more crying. If the trek home hadn't killed him, perhaps all this affection might! He was exhausted and clearly needed something to drink and eat. We sat him down at the kitchen table and the ladies busied themselves preparing bread, butter, and a little bit of wurst (sausage). My aunt handed him a warm beer. It was like a king's banquet. He was in awe. He tried to talk, drink, and eat all at the same time while everyone was shouting questions at him. It was pure chaos, but all in a loving way!

After a few minutes, a hush came over the room as he began to tell us what had happened to him and how he'd made it home. Toward the end of the war, he had been sent with his unit from France to Belgium, marching the whole way. At that point, food and ammunition were in short supply. The sense that the war was nearing the end was prevalent among the ranks, although no one came right out and said as much. But dread was the emotion that dominated their minds.

They encountered the enemy as they entered Brussels. Fighting was intense and brutal. No matter what his men did, they couldn't penetrate the city. Scores of soldiers lay dead or wounded all around him. After three days of constant battle, he was hit with shrapnel from an exploding grenade that killed three men next to him. He ended up in a hospital with a wound to his head and minor penetrating wounds in his arms and legs. His hospital was captured by the Americans soon thereafter.

After an hour or so into this reunion, it was clear that everyone was tired and wanted to retire for the night. They also wanted to give some time and privacy to the newly rejoined couple.

I vividly remember sleeping with a few of my cousins that night, and for several more nights after that!

After a day or two, stories of my father's exploits during the war started to become commonplace, first as a trickle and then as a flood, since he was eager to share. I sensed that it was like therapy for him.

One story stuck in my mind because it illustrated what kind of person my father was and detailed the perils of warfare from the German side. He was one of the youngest sergeants in the German army and quickly rose through the ranks to become a lieutenant. He was in charge of a company of about 120 men. He was an excellent leader and all the men under his leadership liked and respected him.

One autumn day near the French/Belgium border about six months before the war ended, his unit captured six French partisan fighters. They were armed but dressed in civilian clothing. Dad was in charge of questioning them, standing in the middle of a town square, surrounded by his company and the French interpreter.

Suddenly, out of nowhere, an SS jeep turned the corner. A major, dressed all in black, with knee-high boots polished to a sheen, jumped out of the passenger seat, followed by a couple of lieutenants. The major briskly walked over to my father and in a very authoritative tone demanded to know what was going on.

"Who are these men, and what are you interrogating them for?"

My father replied, "We captured these partisans, we are still questioning them. They haven't given us much and we don't know what to do with them yet."

The major commanded with authority, "Just shoot them!"

My father replied, "Sir, with all due respect, I cannot do that."

The major turned to his officers and yelled, "Shoot the lieutenant, and then shoot the prisoners!"

My father froze as two officers pulled their Lugers out from their holsters. Before the dutiful lieutenants could raise their pistols to shoulder height, a loud series of clicks broke the silence. The entire company surrounding my father and the six French partisans cocked their rifles and aimed them at the four SS officers. 120 rifles pointing directly at these officers fighting on the same side!

The blood drained from the major's face as he realized what was about to happen. He apparently got the message. The SS officers slowly holstered their pistols. The commanding officer barked out an order and hurriedly jumped back into his jeep, signaling his entourage to leave.

As the jeep pulled away, he yelled out the window, "I will be back shortly to deal with you!" as he pointed at Dad.

My father knew what that meant. SS officers did not take insubordination and disrespect like that lightly. He and all of his men were now in danger. Their fate was the firing squad if they didn't act quickly.

He instructed the partisans to disappear into the woods (it was their lucky day, too) and then yelled at his men to hoof it out of town double-time! They all understood they had to make themselves scarce before the SS soldiers returned with reinforcements. The SS officer was never heard from again.

A few months later, my dad was wounded. Shrapnel from an exploding round hit him right between the eyes and he experienced a few glancing blows to his arms and legs. He was lucky. Although the wound from his head bled profusely, it appeared to be superficial. His head was bandaged in such a way that he could just barely see out of one eye.

He was relieved of his duties and put in charge of about twenty wounded soldiers in a small burned out church, haphazardly transitioned into a hospital. Since he was the only one mobile yet was too wounded to fight, he was left behind as the officer in charge. The German army was now in full retreat. He was instructed to wait for the advancing enemy US army to arrive and then surrender himself, the wounded soldiers, and the hospital as a whole. The wounded were lying on straw and leaves, and they were left with no medication or food.

Three days passed uneventfully. There was no action at all. His soldiers were in bad shape, now even thirstier and hungrier. Late in the afternoon on the third day, the silence was broken by the sound of rotor tracks. A tank with a white star on both sides stopped in front of the makeshift hospital, which was flying a white flag indicating that the Germans inside were surrendering. A couple of American soldiers entered with their rifles pointed. After they saw all the wounded, one yelled, "All clear!" and a lieutenant entered with a couple more soldiers by his side.

One of the Americans asked quite loudly in German, "Who is in charge?"

My father stepped forward and saluted.

Dad replied with his name, rank, and serial number as was protocol. He then reported that they were all wounded and offered to surrender peacefully. The American lieutenant, through his interpreter, asked what the wounded needed. My father told him bandages, food, water, and if they could spare it, some cigarettes.

The young American lieutenant barked out some orders to his men. They left and returned minutes later, carrying a few boxes of supplies. They followed the lieutenant as he walked from one wounded man to another, throwing C-rations and a pack of cigarettes into the lap of each and every wounded soldier. He then let my father know that he was to wait for the second stage of the invasion to arrive. It might be a few days before the rear echelon reached the church. The second wave would then officially take them as prisoners.

As the Americans started to leave, my father stood up once again and saluted the lieutenant. The lieutenant, just as officially, saluted him back, a clear show of respect from both sides. Later, my father told me how impressed he was by this man--not only his professionalism, but how polite and courteous he was after taking control of this beleaguered hospital.

He was now officially a POW. His men had hoped that if they were to be captured, it would be at the hands of the Americans. Fortunately, their wish was granted. As promised, the second wave of American troops arrived at the hospital about four days later. This unit was just as respectful and obliging as the first. They prepped the wounded to be moved to a POW camp about twenty clicks away. As the undertaking was slow-going, the journey took almost twelve hours.

Not long after Papa was captured, the war ended. There was a quiet celebration among the POWs, and while their captors went on an all-night bender of drink and merriment, the US soldiers shared the jubilation with the the POWs, too.

In processing his papers and during subsequent investigations, the American interrogators learned that although Papa was an enemy combatant, he was sworn in during the Hindenburg regime and not Hitler's. He was therefore not considered a Nazi and was released.

The POW camp was just south of Brussels, Belgium. Almost comically, the gates were opened and he was let go with nothing more than the clothes on his back and no instructions on what to do next. So he started walking in the direction he thought Germany was, due southeast. At times, he was able to explain his plight and hitch a ride with a US medical or logistical transport. But for the most part, he just walked. Another challenge was that the area was still transitioning through the early stages of disarmament and he kept getting picked up by GIs who thought he was an escaped POW. Inexplicably, he always managed to talk his way out of it.

It took almost six weeks and 350 miles of persistence, but with good luck and fortune he just showed up at home that memorable night.

The hurdles facing my parents were innumerable. First and foremost was that, even though I was now ten and they'd been officially married five years before, they had hardly spent any time together. They needed to get to know each other again.

With no job and no place to live, my father had to ask my mother's parents if he could move in with them. It meant even tighter quarters, since my grandmother's sisters and all their children still lived there, too.

After a few weeks, Dad was having a hard time finding a job, so he went back to the trade he had learned as a teen--upholstery. Since many people had partly burned or damaged sofas and chairs that needed repair, business was very good. He worked in the attic, and I helped him, especially with carrying the heavy pieces of furniture up and down the stairs.

Not having a dad for the first ten years of my life made the transition a bit difficult. I was used to doing whatever I wanted. But even though he was very strict and he made his will known, it was good to have a dad again. I enjoyed sitting with him in the evening and listening to his war stories.

My parents were also faced the challenge of living together and finally forming a family unit. Just a few months after my father returned, my mother announced that she was pregnant. In hindsight, you could almost surmise that my sister was conceived the very first night he returned. She was a welcome home present!

After the happy announcement, my parents realized they had to find a place of their own. Our current living conditions were just too cramped. They soon learned that finding a place to rent was practically impossible. Bombing victims and refugees from the east were given priority. My father became more and more frustrated in his search. He felt that putting bombing victims first was totally unfair.

He used to say, "I stuck my neck out and fought in the war and got wounded, and now that I'm back home I can't get a job or find a decent place to live."

He even went to the see the mayor, but to no avail. The only solution was for us to move in with his mother for a few months, since she was living alone and had more than enough room. As the housing authority began to loosen its rules, my grandmother was given priority a few months later and was provided with a smaller flat about two blocks away. As a result, by early 1946, we finally had our own place.

It was a good thing, too, since my mother gave birth to my sister Christa in April of 1946. Fortune started to swing in our direction. About a month later, the city of Nuremberg announced the restart of the city police force. Papa applied and was immediately accepted. What more could we ask for?

Being the son of a policeman like my dad was no easy position. My father was very stringent with his rules. He would always say, "Son, don't embarrass me or your family."

He made sure I associated myself with well-behaved boys from respectable families. Having a father back in my life was a mixed blessing. As stern as he was, he restored order like the army officer that had been ingrained into him. I had to observe a strict curfew. This was especially hard for me since before and after the war, I had been free to roam throughout the city at all hours of day and night. God forbid I came home a few minutes late and broke curfew. Boy, did I pay the price.

Even after I turned fourteen and worked a full forty-eight hours per week as a tool and die maker apprentice, I still had to be home by 7 pm on weekdays and 9 pm on Saturdays. This curfew even lasted until my last day in Germany, when I was seventeen and wanted to spend my last night saying goodbye to my girlfriend before I left for America.

He demanded, "Remember, be home by 9."

I was so upset!

My mother intervened, imploring him, "Come on, Hans. It's his last day in Germany. Give the boy a break. He wants to give his girlfriend a proper goodbye."

My dad weakened and said, "Okay, be home by 11!"

The next day, I left Nuremburg by train for Hamburg, and the new life that was about to start for me.

CHAPTER TWENTY-TWO

The Land of Milk and Honey

Why America? Despite the Allies' efforts to re-build Germany, its economy in general, and Nuremberg specifically, progress was exceedingly slow, especially for someone like me who had bigger plans. You could say I had wanderlust.

I was able to see a lot of Germany in the post-war era. When I turned fourteen in 1949, I was hired as a tool and die apprentice. I had a head for math and I was perfect for the job, since a lot of precise calculations went into producing machine parts. The demand for this work was critical in helping rebuild the country. However, during the summer months back in those days, it was too hot to work in the machine shops. The solution was rotating holidays. Although the shop didn't close, we were required to take mandatory time off. I always chose the month of August for my vacation since it was the hottest and it was my birthday month.

During my holidays, I, along with two of my best friends from work, would ride our bicycles as far as our legs would take us. We would normally work six days per week, so on Sundays we could only take short biking trips from town to town, searching for our next adventure. But with a month off, we had more time to explore. Every summer for three years, we would each pack a bed roll and a change of clothes (we only had two sets) and off we would go. We pedaled all over West Germany, witnessing all its splendor as it was being rebuilt. Needless to say, we met our fair share of the opposite sex, too. These trips transformed us from boys to men as we were forced to negotiate through all of life's challenges on the road. Keeping our wits about us while managing both the good and the bad required a lot of growing up.

But as we saw the country, I became acutely aware that substantial economic hardships persisted. Running water and indoor plumbing were still not universally available. In fact, personal hygiene in most places was only accomplished by utilizing the public baths. It was so expensive that it only made financial sense to go once a week, typically on Saturday. The luxury of a bath cost at least 25% of our weekly wages.

There were other economic hurdles, as well. Food availability, although improving, was still limited to what local farms could afford to grow or the country could import. The transportation system, including rail and road, was slowly being rebuilt. I just wasn't convinced that prospering in Germany was a real possibility. Another reason I felt compelled to leave home was the impact made by my positive interactions with the GIs during and after the war. They made quite an impression on me. The GIs always comported themselves with self-assuredness and dignity. In my eyes, America held real promise.

Most importantly, there were the stories circulating of finding one's fame and fortune in the new world. As portrayed in the movies, as well as in the papers, there were endless possibilities in America. Freedom and opportunity were at the top of my mind. America was clearly the land of milk and honey, and I wanted to go.

To top it all off, we actually had family in America. In 1920, shortly after World War I, my paternal grandfather's brother Jakob Bayer (Uncle Jack) left Germany, first for Canada and then ultimately landing in New

York. He married a fellow German girl (Aunt Mary) once he got there. Together, they had one son (cousin Jackie) and made a good life in New York City.

Since mail was a scarcity, we never had any real contact with them during the war. Coinciding with the end of the war and the reestablishment of shipping lines in the summer of 1945, we started to receive care packages from our newfound family in America. For years, we would get a monthly care package filled with sugar, coffee, milk, chocolate, cigarettes, clothes, and shoes. We were thrilled beyond comprehension. Our gratitude was neverending. My growing interest in all things American was piqued.

Due to a lack of communication, some of the gifts were comical. For example, it was difficult to translate shoe sizes between the two countries, so the shoes and sneakers I received were either too small or too big. But out of necessity, I wore them anyway, despite the fact that my feet hurt all the time if they were too small and I looked like a clown if they were too big.

My father and my uncle must have discussed futbol (soccer) in one letter. However, the message was clearly misunderstood, since one care package contained an American football. You should have seen my face when I opened that one. But boys being boys meant we had to try it. Imagine watching twelve kids running around a park trying to play soccer with a football. The ball never bounced the way it was expected. We had no idea how to play with it. After a few futile games, we stopped kicking it and started to throw it around the neighborhood. Little did we know we were finally utilizing it correctly.

When you turn fourteen in Germany, you are expected to be confirmed in the faith of the family, which for me was Lutheran. The problem was that I had no clothes suitable for confirmation. I wrote to Uncle Jack about my dilemma, and a few weeks later, I received a package containing a navy pinstripe suit, paisley tie, white shirt, and brown wing tip shoes. I was now able to attend my confirmation in style. I was forever grateful.

After learning about my familial connection to America, my imagination ran wild thinking what it would be like to live in New York City. We made sure to send proper thank-you notes and letters to my uncle and aunt on a regular basis and reported on what life was like in Germany. I was also ecstatic to learn that I had a cousin who was just a little older than I. He was named for his father Jack, but in his younger years he went by Jackie. He and I became pen pals, exchanging letters every few weeks. I caught a glimpse of what life in America was like and I shared with him about all my adventures in re-building Germany. As we continued to communicate, they began sending me more of my cousin's hand-me-down clothing as he outgrew them. I think I piqued his interest in Germany, too.

In May of 1951, Jackie wrote that he was graduating high school and for a graduation present, he'd requested a trip to Germany, and his father had agreed. He asked if he could spend a week or two with me and my family. We were thrilled, and of course we said yes. In late July, we welcomed Jackie into our humble and small home. He got to share my bedroom, sleeping on a make-shift bed on the floor. Although he was two years older than me, he and I hit it off right away. Jackie was quite fluent in German, having learned it at home, and I knew a few important words in English that I'd learned from the GIs.

My factory was on holiday, so I was able to show him the sights. Although the rebuilding process had started, the city still lay in all forms of ruin. It was normal for us at this point, but it was somewhat of a shock for Jackie. I took him to all the famous tourist spots, including the castle, the churches, and all the popular watering holes, introducing him to some authentic German beer. Many a night we stumbled home drunk, holding each other up and quickly becoming each other's new best friend. I believe the highlight of his trip was on his first Saturday when I took him down to the lake to swim and sunbathe. He had no idea German girls sunbathed topless. The liberal German culture certainly appealed to him.

During his second week with us, my mother asked him, "After having eaten all this German food for the last week, would you like something American?"

He grinned and said, "That would be fantastic."

Mama asked, "What would he like?"

"Steak!" was his reply.

Since beef was in short supply and cows were meant for milking, she didn't really know what steak was. Mama promptly went to the butcher and ordered it. She came home with quarter inch fillets, each about a pound.

Not knowing any better, she asked, "Jackie, should I fry them in a frying pan for 15 minutes on each side?"

Jackie almost choked with laughter and said, "God, no. Four minutes on each side will be more than enough!"

My mom turned to me and whispered, "Boy, all these Americans like to eat their meat raw." I smiled.

But she followed his directions, and I must say...my first steak was delicious!

We spent almost two weeks together. He got to spend time with not only my family but with the entire extended family. He truly garnered a better understanding of his roots during his visit. We really became fast friends, and perhaps after two weeks, even more like brothers than cousins. Neither of us wanted the holiday to end.

When the time came to pack up, Jackie asked me the question that would change my life. "Would you ever be interested in coming to America, and not just for a visit, but to live?"

Without hesitation, I answered with a resounding, "Yes!"

He said when he got home he would ask his parents to sponsor me. I was on top of the world. But how would I break it to my parents?

At that time, to emigrate to America, you had to have a sponsor, someone who would vouch for your moral integrity and financial wellbeing. This was a big favor to ask, and I was immediately grateful for the offer. But it was up to Uncle Jack and Aunt Mary, and that was not a guarantee.

Two weeks after Jackie returned, a letter arrived with bad news. Jack explained that he told his parents all about me and my desire to come to America. Unfortunately, his parents had had a bad experience sponsoring a nephew on Aunt Mary's side, and therefore would not be in favor of repeating the same mistake and sponsoring another immigrant from Germany.

Just like that, my dreams of going to America were over before they'd even started. As a backup plan, I was contemplating an option to sign up with a large manufacturing company with options to to go to South Africa or Australia on a five-year contract and work as a master tool and die maker following the completion of my apprenticeship. It sounded very promising and exciting.

I wrote back to Jack. I said I understood his parent's decision and went on to explain that I could go to two other countries instead. Before I could sign anything official, a week later a letter arrived from Jackie, begging me to not consider going to South Africa or Australia but to come to America instead. He had changed his father's mind. Jackie had convinced him that I was a viable candidate for sponsorship. He'd said I had a practical skill, and I was respectful and hardworking. Apparently, it worked.

I hadn't yet broken the news of any of these options to my parents. When I did, my father was elated and my mother was crestfallen. Inconsolable was more like it.

Although I understood my mother's sorrow, this was my opportunity to realize my goals.

I decided right then and there in August of 1952 that this was my future. However, I was still only sixteen years old. Of course, my parents had to sign off on this crazy idea. My apprenticeship would end in May of 1953, so I had about ten months to plan and get my passport, my visa, and my act together. In September, I took a day off from work and went to the American Consulate to apply for that visa. I spent the entire day in the immigration department, being ushered to various desks, answering questions, and filling out forms. Finally, late that day, I was told that I was done and a visa would be issued within a year.

The following March, my visa arrived by mail. It only took six months. My father and I were proud, but my mother cried inconsolably. She later confessed that she'd been tempted to burn it, since she was the one who'd found the envelope. Luckily, my father came home and stopped her.

I immediately wrote to my uncle with the good news and in no time, he answered me back. He informed me that an international money order of $300 would be sent to me and I should book a ship's passage at my earliest convenience. In what seemed like the blink of an eye, everything fell into place…the money arrived and I went to a travel agency and booked my passage. I was to sail on the SS Italia, which was scheduled to leave Hamburg on June 20, 1953.

The ship was built in 1928 and originally launched as the MS Kungsholm. In 1948 she was re-christened the SS Italia and served as the premier North Atlantic liner of the Swedish American Line. For sixteen years, she would bring countless immigrants from all over Europe to America, ending her reign in 1964. She was one of the more majestic ships of her day, and she was my salvation!

Things were quickly getting serious. As my parents and I took stock of my clothes, my mother shrieked and said, "I can't have my son going to America in these used rags!" Jack's hand-me-downs had dried up as I grew to be a bit bigger than he.

They took inventory of my wardrobe and realized I had very little to wear. They discussed it together and decided to buy me some new clothes. They determined what was needed and how much it would cost. It didn't take long to come to the conclusion that they didn't have enough money. So heavyhearted, my dad decided we would need to take out a loan. With the money he borrowed, I was able to get a woolen suit, a spring jacket, a pair of slacks, a pair of shoes, a new razor, and various toiletries. One thing we forgot to buy was new underwear. There was even enough left over for a suitcase. I am forever grateful to both of my parents not only for making this happen by going into debt but for letting me go in the first place. It was a true sacrifice. I would learn over time that it was the ultimate price a parent makes for a child— to let them stretch their wings and fly.

Within the next month, I acquired a German passport, the last piece of the puzzle. I was ready to go. The day finally came when I had to say goodbye to my mother and nine-year-old sister. To say there was a river of tears would be an understatement. I hugged both of them for what felt like hours. Neither wanted to let go.

My father and I decided to leave the day before the sailing date because he was able to get us a ride from a friend in a semi-truck of a local transportation company instead of having to pay for train fare. As a police officer, he had many connections.

When we got to Hamburg, it all became real! The hardest thing I ever did was stand on that pier, hug my father, and say, "Goodbye, Papa!"

And if it was hard for me, I can't imagine for a moment how hard it was for him to say goodbye to me. He had missed the first ten years of my life fighting in the war. Then he got to know me over the next seven years, and we even became friends. Now he was letting me leave to live my best life! It was the purest form of unconditional love I will ever know. He was a special man! Even though the time we had together was short, the quality cannot be taken for granted. That is what he gave me...quality. He was and will forever be my hero. He was the ideal of a man I spent my entire life trying to live up to. .

CHAPTER TWENTY-THREE

Give Me Your Tired, Your Poor, Your Huddled Masses...

Before I could get too sentimental, I was swiftly immersed in ship life. I grew up almost instantly.

I had never been on a ship before, so it was very exciting for me to spend the next few days exploring. My passage cost $275. Therefore, I had $25 leftover, which my mother promptly pinned to the inside of my underwear. Truth be told, time had elapsed too quickly before they could buy me underwear, so I was actually wearing the only pair of underwear my mother owned! True story!!

The food on board was fantastic, given that I was still limited in my culinary choices back home. I must have put on ten pounds. I was assigned to a table of ten young men just like myself, about to forge our way in the new frontier. We all became fast friends and caroused together the whole time. Despite the festive mood on board and the nonstop partying, during the entire 10-day passage, I spent only $5, and most of that was on beer. Therefore, when I arrived in America, all I had to my name was my new suit, two pair of slacks, three shirts, a suitcase, and $20.

As with all immigrants in the 20th century, our ship sailed into New York City, passing the Statue of Liberty. It was a memory above all memories! The notion of being welcomed with open arms as a displaced citizen was beyond belief!

Just about every passenger stood on the upper deck, witnessing our arrival into the New York harbor. You could have heard a quarter drop on the deck. It was that quiet and reverent as we passed Lady Liberty herself.

The feeling of elation I was experiencing was beyond my wildest imagination. Standing on that ship, staring up, first at the bronzed symbol of freedom followed by these majestic buildings, was surreal. It was a city that beckoned me. I had only heard of such promise and potential but I knew I was in the land of milk and honey.

We sailed up the Hudson, guided by two powerful tug boats, on July 1, 1953, arriving at 11 am and docking at Pier 94 on the west side of Manhattan. I was home!

After the formalities of disembarkation, including passing a medical exam and clearing customs, I was met at the pier by my New York family, my uncle, aunt, and cousin. They stood there with big smiles on their faces and held a bouquet of flowers.

I was fully embraced in hugs of freedom and opportunity.

I was whisked off to their home in a brand-new black Buick sedan. Their home was in Queens, one of the five boroughs of New York City. They lived in Rego Park in an attached brick house in a working-class neighborhood. After living in a bombed-out city still struggling to rebuild, I thought this place was beautiful.

The house was filled with neighbors and friends, all of whom were German immigrants, too. My uncle and aunt had not completely given up on their German roots. In fact, they were the founding members of a German folk-dancing (*Schuplattler*) club called the *Gemuetlichen*

Enzianer. Many members of this club were at my uncle and aunt's house my first day to greet me and share in my first American meal. Well, it was my inaugural dinner, but the table was loaded with all the traditional German food I could think of, including various types of sausages, marinated beef (*Sauerbraten*), red cabbage, sauerkraut, and potato dumplings and gravy, with a a traditional apple struedel for dessert. What a welcome!

After all the food and German beer I could consume, I was full and exhausted. I went to sleep for the first time under the flag of my new country.

I woke the next morning, greeted by an oppressive heatwave. I sweat right through my t-shirt and shorts. It gets warm in Germany, but not like what I experienced in New York that first weekend. It was 95 degrees with 90% humidity. Fortunately, I was told the night before that we would be taking a trip in the morning to the "country," as leaving the confines of New York City in the summer was called back then. This German-American club that I'd been welcomed into the night before had a clubhouse, or "Alpine house," on Lake Secor, about 50 miles north of the city in the town of Mahopac. We were going to spend the 4th of July weekend enjoying more merriment in the bosom of German culture once again.

It took us about an hour to make the drive in my uncle's car. I didn't have a wardrobe that would meet the demands of this heat. All I had to wear were wool trousers and a long-sleeved cotton shirt. I was dripping from the moment we left the house. Thankfully, it was a bit cooler in the woods along the lake.

I was completely taken aback by the clubhouse once we unloaded the suitcases. The club members had thought of everything when they'd built the house twenty years earlier. It looked like a hut you would find in the German Alps. The first floor was a big party room with a fully stocked bar and galley kitchen. Despite it only being about 1,500 square feet, the house could sleep forty people. Comfort, however, was in the eye of the beholder.

This was possible because the women slept on the second floor in three separate bedrooms and the men slept in the attic. The beds were army-issued bunks for the women and cots with horse-hair matresses for the men. I figured that comfort was not a priority once I saw how much everyone drank. It was a matter of passing out rather than sleeping. And fire safety didn't seem to be of much concern.

We spent the holiday weekend playing volleyball and horseshoes by day and drinking, eating, and dancing to accordian music by night. These first few days were amazing, and I immediately applied for membership in this terrific organization. This club influenced the rest of my life. It became my social connection, has led to many new friendships, and helped me get the first job in my chosen trade. I wasn't in the country a week, and I now had lifelong friends named Hugo, Kurt, Marianne, Alex, and my cousin Jackie, to just name a few.

When we returned to New York City upon the completion of the weekend, I drew up a plan to learn English and get a job. I taught myself English by reading the newspaper while checking unknown words in a dictionary, and watching TV. In September, I enrolled in an eight-week English class at night.

Someone in the club had a connection to small manufacturing company owned by a fellow German who immediately hired me. I was working by the middle of

July, making twice as much as I'd been making in Germany.

Through the club, I was also introduced to a soccer team that played in Ridgewood, Queens, which was predominately made up of German immigrants. The club was called *Eintracht*. I would play soccer and be involved with various German soccer clubs for many years to come. My immersion in the New York City scene was complete.

Soccer introduced me to my future wife. My first autumn after my arrival in New York, I met this beautiful young woman whom I spotted watching our soccer game with five of her girlfriends. It was a freezing morning in late fall of 1953, so I assumed they must all have been huge fans. The truth was a bit more contrived. Her Uncle Willie, a fellow Bavarian, was the soccer fan, and he attended every game we played. He mentioned to his niece and all her young girlfriends that a bunch of young German boys were playing soccer every Sunday and suggested that they join him. Despite the frigid weather, they all came as a pack.

After that first game, I met Marianne Hauck and her friends. Uncle Willie invited us all back to his house once we'd had a chance to shower. Five teammates and I jumped at the chance.

We traveled ten minutes to Astoria, Queens and met Marianne's family. We were all very comfortable, given that everyone there spoke German. Marianne and I hit it off immediately. We started dating the following week. And each one of my friends paired up, too. Ironically, Uncle Willie was responsible for at least six marriages that day!

I was fully embracing my assimilation into the American way of life. I even took drum lessons to increase my chances of making a living, as German bands in the '50s were quite popular, playing at Oktoberfests and various German affairs all year around.

I had a great job, a beautiful girlfriend, a large group of German friends from the dance and soccer club, as well as a swelling bank account.

CHAPTER TWENTY-FOUR

Back To Germany as an American

Life was progressing according to my plan. But despite my admitted happiness and success, I was growing homesick, which a lot of immigrants naturally experience. Because of my fondness for the American soldiers and the ideals they represented, and the advice of my uncle, I enlisted in the US army in 1955, hoping for a chance to be stationed back in Germany.

I spent ten weeks in boot camp at Fort Knox, Kentucky, and later a short stint at Fort Dix, New Jersey. I had never really encountered discrimination, either aimed at my direction as an immigrant or witnessed it focused on anyone of color.

When I got to Fort Knox, that all changed, especially as I tried to go to a drugstore lunch counter with a fellow New York soldier/friend of mine named Ernie Brooks, who was black. It struck me square in the face when he said he couldn't sit next to me since there was a "Blacks Only" section at the back of the resturant. As an alternative, I naively suggested I join him in "his" section. Before he could object, the manager overheard the conversation and loudly demanded that we both leave the establishment, screaming at us, "I won't serve no nigger lovers!"

We were both soldiers, wearing our uniforms, serving and protecting our country respectfully and honorably. I couldn't wrap my head around what we had done wrong to be treated with such disdain. Once we were clear of the restaurant, Ernie explained the facts of life of being a black soldier in the Jim Crow south. Being that he, too, was from New York, he was at a loss to figure it out since discrimination wasn't as overt in the northeast, but just as real. From then on I was more acutely aware of the perils of prejudice and the irony as it relates to the freedom and liberty for all that I was seeking.

Once boot camp was completed, after a short stop in New Jersey, I was fortunate to be stationed back in Germany as I had hoped. Given my bilingual talents, I spent two years working as a tank and jeep driver for the various base commanders in Mannheim. It was only a three-hour drive or train ride to Nuremburg, so I was able to spend almost every weekend with my family.

It was a special time in my life as I was able to re-kindle my relationship with my parents and get to know my now nine-year-old sister. Naturally, my mother was thrilled with my proximity and frequent visits. My father was now a sergeant in the Nuremberg police force. And my family was a prominent member of the city. It also gave me the opportunity to bond with my father over many a beer. He came to know me as a man and I could sense the respect and love that he had for me.

Reuniting with Bavarian cuisine was also a good bonus as I could get my fill of the things Nuremberg is known for, including bratwurst (sausage) and lebkuchen (gingerbread).

On one particular train ride home, I was alone in a compartment with a young German couple clearly in love. I was dressed in my Army fatigues, so they thought they were traveling with an American. Halfway through the trip, their romance took a sudden detour as they became embroiled in a very heated and animated argument. They clearly assumed I had no idea what was going on as I feigned sleep. They called each other every name in the book as the gloves came off.

My stop came before theirs, and as I got up to leave, I said in my perfect German, "You two make a nice couple, so whatever your differences are, I hope you work it out. Have a great day."

Well, you could have lifted their jaws off the ground as they were shocked into disbelief that they'd been traveling the whole time with a German-speaking American soldier. Every time I traveled on the train or went out with my buddies, I had an opportunity to mess with German minds when I'd switch from English to German. It always left them with the same dismayed look. It was priceless.

During the latter part of my stint overseas, Marianne and her family booked passage on a ship and made a trip over to Germany, both to visit with their family in their hometown in the Black Forest region and to see me. I earned a four-day pass and jumped on the first train to Neuhaus, just south of Stuttgart.

We had a great visit. Shockingly, the regional dialect of her family who lived there was almost imperceptible to me. We were all speaking German, but you never would have known it. At the end of our time together, I knew more than ever that Marianne was the one for me. It would be another year before we were reunited.

I would earn an honorable discharge after serving my adopted country for two memorable years. I then returned to the States in 1957. Between my army savings, my lucrative new job since returning, and moonlighting on weekends playing drums in a number of German bands, I knew I could build a good life for the two of us. On February 14, 1958, Valentine's day, I proposed to Marianne and she accepted straight away. We were married on September 25, 1960, in front of 150 friends and family. My parents had only enough money for my mother to attend. I'm sure my father was greatly disappointed, but my mother went home with a full roll of pictures to share with him.

First, we moved to Irvington, NY, the blossoming suburbs of New York City. Not long afterward, I got a job with IBM in the Hudson Valley, requiring us to move north, first to Hawthorne, NY, and then on to Mahopac, NY, in 1970. Ironically, Mahopac was the very same town where I'd spent my first weekend in the states, just five miles from Lake Secor and the clubhouse. It was kismet!

I knew getting a bachelor's degree would be beneficial in my career pursuits. Attending school exclusively at night, I received my degree in mechanical engineering from Farleigh Dickinson University in 1972. It took me almost nine years, but I refused to give up. All the while, I worked 50 hours per week and either danced with the club on the weekends, played in the band, or both.

My greatest accomplishment was fathering three boys in eight years. Gregory came in 1961, Christopher in 1965, and Mark in 1969. They would all go on to be successful in their own right. Greg owns a wealth management firm, Chris is an assistant superintendent of a city school district, and Mark is a high school principal. I have been given the priceless gift of watching my three grandchildren grow to adulthood, as well.

As for the German club, it would be a relationship that would last for a lifetime. I would be elected president of our club and be awarded lifetime honorary officer positions. A few of my fellow members and I even became minor celebrities by appearing on the *Tonight Show Starring Johnny Carson* in 1971 when it was still filmed in New York City, performing our traditional dance. The president of our club at the time, Marty Hubner, sat with Johnny in the guest chair, and Johnny even donned his tradional German hat.

During my time in the make-up chair before the show, I sat next to Maureen Stapleton, the famous actress. She was very interested in my costume and asked me a lot of questions. She was an absolute gem.

Dancing also afforded us the opportunity to perform on many cruise ships as they, too, embraced the Oktoberfest theme.

I know it made my father proud when I became an officer in the national organization (*Gauverband North America*) governing the eighty or so traditional German clubs across the US. I would help coordinate the prize dancing for many years at our biannual conventions. It also took me back to my homeland many times, as we forged friendships with several of the original clubs in Germany. My father got to witness his son and grandsons uphold tradition and dance in Bavaria, as well. My life had come full circle.

I enjoyed a successful 25 year career at IBM (I was euphemistically called the father of ion implantation, having secured a number of patents), retiring in 1986. I went on to found a company called Support Systems, Inc., with two locations, one in East Fishkill, New York, and the other in Austin, Texas. We provided high-tech decontaminating services for my former employer and other semiconductor companies such as DuPont, Applied Materials, Lam Research, Motorola, Intel, and AMD. At our peak, we employed over 80 people.

The industry began to consolidate in the '90s and only the strong would survive. The market was ripe. I sold the company in 1998 to a publicly-traded firm from Columbus, Ohio, for a tidy sum.

I enjoyed my second retirement by buying a house in a golfing community in Naples, Florida. It was also a popular destination for all my friends from the various German clubs in New York who also happened to move there. Marianne and I hosted many an Oktoberfest or accordian fest at out house with well over 50 friends from back home. It was not uncommon for the crowd to arrive before noon to the sound of accordian music, the smell of German sausages on the barbeque, and the free-flowing of a barrel of beer.

In July of 2008, Marianne and I were fortunate to be able to take the entire family, including my three grandchildren, on a riverboat cruise, ten of us all together. The tour began in Budapest and we spent seven days floating down the Danube river. The trip culminated in Nuremberg where we spent another seven days taking it in as a tourist. It was dream of mine to show off my hometown to my family so they could have pictures to go with all the stories I told over the years. We visited all the sites from my childhood, including the old apartment we sheltered in during the war, the church where I snagged the brass cross, as well as the castle. We feasted on Nuremberger bratwurst and beer.

We also spent some real quality time with my sister Christa, her husband Ludwig, and my cousin Marichen who I grew up with during the war. It was a trip of a lifetime. I literally lived the American dream I had in my mind when I was seventeen years old!

CHAPTER TWENTY-Five

FATE

And just to cement how fate works, my father's war experience in WWII would follow me to America.

In 1967, now married for six years, with two children and living in Hawthorne, New York, my parents and younger sister came for a summer visit. We lived in a typical, bucolic neighborhood of about twenty-five homes just thirty miles north of New York City. We were part of the growing trend of the mass exodus from the city to the suburbs. One of our neighbors, Fred and Mary Johnson, had heard about the pending arrival of my family. In the three years we'd lived there, Fred and I had shared war stories. He, being twenty or so years older than me, shared his experiences fighting in the war, and I contributed my exploits as a boy trying to survive the war. I brought to life some of my father's war stories, too. Just after my family arrived, Fred insisted on hosting a party in their honor.

He explained that during his tour of duty, he met many German soldiers of distinction. He said that even though he fought against the German army as an American officer, he had a tremendous amount of reverence for the German soldier.

On the appointed day, we all walked to Fred and Mary's house. After some short introductions, I began to translate for the two men and explain each other's role and respective locations in the war. Within about five minutes it became incredibly clear that Fred was the US lieutenant my father had met in that Belgium hospital and had ultimately surrendered to!

Talk about a coincidence. Two men representing their respective armies during the most monumental war in history, once respectful adversaries, only to cross paths once again in a small hamlet in upstate New York.

Not much more than ten minutes later, together, the two men got raucously drunk. Inexplicably, they no longer needed me to translate their conversation for the remainder of the evening. They figured out a way to communicate without using words. They had a ball. Talk about fate!

Epilogue

My dad, Erich Bayer, died November 4, 2016. But just as he lived, his death was no ordinary event.

He was a healthy man for most of his life. But the malnutrition of his youth, coupled with the fatty nature of a German/American diet, started to catch up to him. He began to suffer the ill-effects of cardiovascular disease in his early 70s and had to endure a number of vascular surgeries in Manhattan. He had a heart attack just before his eightieth birthday. A year later, he was in heart failure. It was seven agonizing weeks of misdiagnosis and misinformation. However, right after Halloween, it became clear that he would not recover. The medical community agreed that he was slowly dying, and they recommended that we take him home.

Mom was too fragile to take on such a responsibility. With quick and quiet efficiency, I, along with my two brothers, made the arrangements to bring him to Mark's house in Mahopac, NY, on a Thursday morning. A hospital bed was ordered, Hospice was brought in and an aide was hired. We were assured that his passing would be peaceful and painless. More than likely, it would only be a matter of a day or two. Later the same day, the idea was hatched to have a **GOING AWAY PARTY!** All three of us agreed we would send him out in Oktoberfest style.

Arrangements quickly came together as food was ordered, beer and wine were bought, and friends and family invited.

On Friday, family and friends started arriving just after lunch and it seemed the procession never ended. We had Dad's two best friends from his early German club days, Hugo and Dieter, come with their accordions. They played all his favorites as we all meandered in and around the living room that hosted his hospital bed. Close to fifty people came to pay their respects by holding his hand, whispering in his ear, toasting him with a stein of beer, and enjoying a plate of traditional German food. Even though he was unconscious, we knew he was hearing us because the right word from the right friend would occasionally elicit a slight reaction.

Around 6 that evening, we called his sister, Aunt Christa, in Germany. We explained the dire circumstances. She only had a minute to digest this news before we asked her to say her last words to him. We held the phone to his ear. For ten minutes, she consoled him in German and begged him to let go. She explained that his mother and father were waiting for him across the bridge and all he had to do was walk in their direction. Her words made all the difference, as no less than ten minutes after we hung up with her, his breathing became labored. Everyone was called to his bedside. Every person there held hands and prayed while we cumulatively held his hands, as well. All who were near and dear to him were there to witness his last breath.

He died as he had lived...surrounded by all those who loved him. He was truly a man for the ages. I am proud to call him Dad!

Over the years, Dad told us many stories chronicling his experiences growing up during and after World War II. We encouraged him many times to write it all down. On one especially long drive with Dad to Columbus, Ohio, in 1999, I asked him to share his stories again as I taped him. After his death, I was in charge of handling his affairs and paperwork. There, buried among his files, was a small, spiral notebook filled with some of these cryptically written stories and anecdotes. Some I had heard, and some I had not. Mixing his notes with the oral history was the basis for this book, and my attempt to keep him alive. I hope I made him proud, too!

Gregory J. Bayer

Acknowledgments

A project like this does not happen without a team effort. I'd like to thank Kathy Meis, Shilah LaCoe and Shaun Stacy and everyone at Bublish. A special thanks to Shilah for believing in this idea, keeping the project moving forward and always an encouraging word.

I would not have found my way to Bublish without the insight of Cecilia Robinson so thanks for your guidance.

Many people knew and loved my dad but there were a few who I could count on to provide encouragement and feedback so for that I would like to thank Dieter & Rosemarie Link, Bruce & Bobbi Fabricant and Marty & Joyce Flaton. Your unwavering love of my father will always be cherished.

My father's lifelong friends, who are too numerous to count, were always there for him. He shared many a story and beer with his fellow club members who include Joseph (Eleanor) Knabel, Hugo (Marianne) Kiendl, Kurt (Barbara) Mietzner, Marty (Marianne) Hubner, William (Linda) Hubner, George (Lori) Lindner, Tony (Rosie) Graf, Edmund (Maryann) Killian, Richard (Terry) Killian, Richard (Helen) Im, Al (Loretta) Tietz and Rudy (Maria) Eberhardt.

Of course, this entire story does not happen if it were not for his Uncle Jack and Mary Bayer, his sponsors, and cousin Jack and his wife Ronnie who were as much friends as they were family. Our families spent every holiday together for many years. You have our undying love and appreciation.

To Uncle Willie (Paula) Burger who brought so many couples together including my parents. You were truly a matchmaker for the ages. Your love of soccer was the catalyst for so much happiness.

To my mother Marianne, who has been the bedrock of our family. Your love and devotion to dad was an inspiration for all to see. Your 56-year marriage was truly a fairy tale.

To my brothers Chris (Jose) and Mark. We have shared many wonderful things in our lives, including fond memories of Dad, and you guys have always made him proud! You both, along with Jose, are inspiring the youth of today with your pearls of wisdom and by leading by example. Your impacts will be felt by generations to come.

To my children, Reilly (Jourdain), McKenzie and Braedon. You were the shinning light in your grandfather's eyes. You were why he made such a great life here in America. You were his success. Too bad he didn't witness the birth of his first great-grandchild Islan, but I can see Opa's spirit in him.

To the love of my life Crystal. You make our life together so wonderful and you are the foundation upon which our family is built. I love you to the moon and back! A happy wife is a happy life!

Erich H. Bayer 1935-2016

Nuremburg 1935

Nuremburg 1936

My Parents - 1939

My sister Christa – 1951

SS Italia – 1953 Hamburg

SS Italia – Hamburg 1953

SS Italia - 1953

First soccer team – Eintracht – 1953
Queens, NY

Queens, NY, 1954 – Marianne & Erich

Die Gemuetlichen Enzianer Club – Queens, NY - Marianne & Erich - 1957

Bavarian Costume 1957

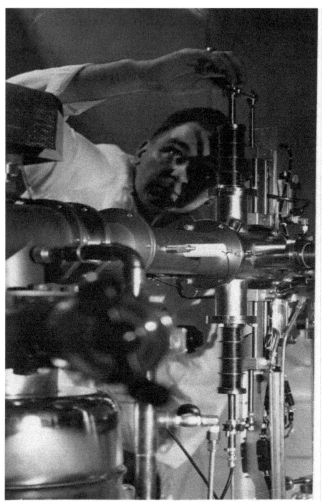

IBM Research 1964 -Yorktown, NY

Uncle Jack & Aunt Mary – Extended family 1981

Mahopac, NY, 1996 – Bayer Family Reunion

Stueben Day Parade Greg, Marianne, & Erich 2015

Family apartment in Nuremburg, 2009

Danube riverboat cruise – 2009

Central Park, NY-Stueben Day Parade - Chris, Mark, & Greg – 2015

Antiqua – 2018 – Brothers forever!

CPSIA information can be obtained
at www.ICGtesting.com
Printed in the USA
LVHW082305050920
665202LV00002B/7